Making a difference?

Exploring the impact of multi-agency working on disabled children with complex health care needs, their families and the professionals who support them

Ruth Townsley, David Abbott and Debby Watson

Family Fund

COMMUNITY FUND

Norah Fry
Research Centre

First published in Great Britain in February 2004 by

The Policy Press
University of Bristol
Fourth Floor, Beacon House
Queen's Road
Bristol BS8 1QU
UK
Tel no +44 (0)117 331 4054
Fax no +44 (0)117 331 4093
E-mail tpp-info@bristol.ac.uk
www.policypress.org.uk

Reprinted 2004

ISBN 1 86134 573 9

British Library Cataloguing in Publication Data
A catalogue record for this report is available from the British Library.

Library of Congress Cataloging-in-Publication Data
A catalog record for this report has been requested.

Ruth Townsley is Senior Research Fellow, **David Abbott** is Research Fellow and **Debby Watson** is Research Fellow, all at the Norah Fry Research Centre, University of Bristol.

The right of Ruth Townsley, David Abbott and Debby Watson to be identified as authors of this work has been asserted by them in accordance with the 1988 Copyright, Designs and Patents Act.

Family Fund
PO Box 50
York YO1 9ZX
www.familyfund.org.uk
t +44 (0)845 130 4542
f +44 (0)1904 652 625

Family Fund

The **Family Fund** champions an inclusive society where families with severely disabled or seriously ill children have choices and the opportunity to enjoy ordinary life.

Cover design by Qube Design Associates, Bristol
Cover illustration © Angela Martin
Printed in Great Britain by Hobbs the Printers Ltd, Southampton

Contents

Preface

The Family Fund champions an inclusive society where families with severely disabled or seriously ill children have choices and the opportunity to enjoy ordinary life. It is particularly fitting that our 30th anniversary should be marked by the publication of *Making a difference?*, commissioned by us from the Norah Fry Research Centre and financed by the Community Fund, which looks at multi-agency working in services to children with complex health care needs. The findings of the study suggest that services have responded well to the health and educational needs of these children. But the overall message from families is that the *ordinariness* of family life is still a long way from being achieved for these children.

Basic rights – to communicate, to develop and maintain relationships, to participate in leisure activities – are not available to the children and young people in this study. The *caring agencies* seem to be overwhelmed by the technology around the child and lose sight of the basics. And carers exhausted by 'keeping the show on the road', and rarely enjoying an uninterrupted night's sleep have few opportunities to *parent* their children in a relaxed and *ordinary* way.

Please read this report, particularly what children and families have to say. Families should be at the heart of the planning, delivery and review processes, at local, regional and national level. But the evidence from this study is that multi-agency working practices exclude parents and carers. The impact of agencies on family life needs to be given paramount consideration and the agencies' primary concern should be the outcome of the arrangements for the child's care on the family as a whole.

And let us keep in mind the breadth of public and private sector agencies and businesses that need to be supported in offering an inclusive service to families. If you do nothing else, ponder on the young man who saw it as his job to make it possible for one family to enjoy a rare moment of enjoyment together:

"We went once to the ice rink and this young man who works there came up to us and said if he got some blankets and put them on a sledge would we like to bring our son on the ice. It was the rarest of moments – all four of us together doing one thing. It made such a difference." (p 46)

This young man is a *champion* for inclusion, just as parents and carers are champions and, as this work shows, many health and social care workers are. Somehow, we have to find ways of harnessing *champions* within an environment that enables and sustains them and encourages the generalisation of their individual enthusiasm and commitment.

We closed down long-stay hospital wards because family life is the right of all children. The responsibility now is to ensure that we do not rebuild the institution within the family.

Marion Lowe
Chief Executive, Family Fund

Bath-time

Having read this report as a parent of a child with complex health care needs, it made me think of a mum in our local support group who said, "It's not the child that's a lot of work, it's the system". How true those words were. Here is a personal example.

Your child needs a bath – quite a straightforward routine for most parents. However, if your child has complex health care needs and is too big to be carried upstairs anymore, what happens?

It was suggested that we take our son five miles to an *accessible bath* – which isn't too bad as long as he doesn't have diarrhoea at 3am! Perhaps we could send someone in to help you? Oh no, he's over the weight limit; they might hurt their back. Anyway is it a *social bath* or a *health bath*? Maybe he could have a bath at school. No success in sorting out school; this is another huge process due to his complex health needs, and besides, that's the education department.

None of these suggestions being any good, it was decided that adaptations had to be made to our house.

Bathing your child then involves – occupational therapists (remember there are social work occupational therapists and health occupational therapists), physiotherapists, paediatricians, nurses, doctors, health visitors, architects, planning department, council, building control, builders, joiners, plumbers, electricians, decorators, social workers, education department, councillors, structural engineers, Citizen's Advice, and so on.

In the meantime we are left frustrated, angry, tired and helpless, phoning *everyone* because if you try *everyone* then surely *someone* will help. It didn't work that way because different departments deal with different issues and have different budgets (although to us the issue was the same). It was clear that something as simple as a child having a bath was causing great stress for everyone. They began to forget that at the heart of this muddle was a *child*.

Eventually the people involved decided that they would need to try and solve this in a new and different way. They decided everyone involved would meet and work *together*! Once they were together they actually discovered they all wanted the same thing. They all wanted this *child* to be able to access a bath. Working together reduced gaps, boundaries and duplication. This was a giant step forward, but the people involved were still stressed and under pressure. Suddenly someone said: "What we need is someone to streamline all of this and feedback to the family. It needs to be someone who knows the *whole family* really well, not just a name".

If coordinating services means reducing gaps, duplication and boundaries, then perhaps what we as families see as obvious, simple and common sense will start to happen. Maybe then we can spend time enjoying our children instead of being exhausted *spinning* around the system.

So the next time you have a bath....

Alison Shankly
Parent of a disabled child with complex health care needs

Acknowledgements

This project has benefited from the time, skills and expertise of a large number of people to whom the research team are very grateful.

As ever, the work would not have been possible without the willingness of parents, carers, children, young people and professionals to meet with us and give us their time and energy. We are especially grateful to all the families and disabled children and young people who met us and took part in our interviews. We hope we have accurately reflected their views and experiences.

Thank you to all the professionals who made time for our interviews and who were frank and thoughtful about their work and the services they provide.

Six services took part in the case-study stage of the research. We were given enormous help in setting up these visits by staff in these services and want to acknowledge the time and effort they put into this as well as the welcome they gave us.

Our research benefited enormously from three advisory groups. Our Research Advisory Group helped us think through many of the challenging aspects of this work and were always helpful and constructive. Thank you to: Obi Amadi, Anette Beattie, Sue Calderwood, Ronny Flynn, Dorothy Hadleigh, Lizzie Hickton, Alvin Jeffs, Sue Kirk, Dot Lawton, Claire Lazarus, Peter Limbrick, Ian Maund, Romola Pocock, Roz Roberts, Carol Robinson, Tracey Roose and Kirsten Stalker.

A Parents Panel met with us over the lifetime of the project and drew on their own very relevant experiences to guide and encourage us. Many thanks to: Kathleen Bebbington, Pauline Flew, Jean Lewis, Mandie Lewis and Angela Shaw.

Emma Brunt and Stuart Talbot formed our young disabled people's group and we are very grateful for the time they gave us to reflect on our interviews with children and young people.

Ian Maund acted as an independent consultant to the project and took the lead on interviews with senior managers, participated in feedback sessions to case-study areas and chaired our Research Advisory Group meetings. We are grateful to him for his expertise and good company over our weeks of fieldwork. Dot Lawton, formerly at the Social Policy Research Unit at the University of York provided us with valuable data from the Family Fund database. Bernie Kelly and Paula Latham helped us with our research interviews.

Our colleagues and commissioners at the Family Fund have been incredibly supportive of this research. Thank you to Marion Lowe, Alison Cowen, Linda Stubbs, Rena Martin, Carole Meikle, Miranda Parrott and Roger Mattingly.

We routinely work as a team at the Norah Fry Research Centre. We are especially grateful to Karen Gyde, Linda Holley, Linda Ward and Sammantha Cave for all their support and hard work through the lifetime of this project.

Finally we are grateful to the Community Fund for supporting this research project.

Executive summary

Disabled children with complex health care needs routinely require support from a wide range of professionals. Many services have been established throughout the UK that aim to implement better joint working between agencies and professionals. The Family Fund in collaboration with the Norah Fry Research Centre wanted to explore what impact multi-agency services had on the lives of this group of children, their families and the professionals that support them. Working closely with six multi-agency services, the researchers found that:

- The six multi-agency services included in this research were providing effective, focused support to families in terms of managing their children's complex health care needs at home. All except one of the children included in this study were living at home, and all those who were of school age were attending a local school or nursery on a regular basis. These findings appear to indicate that multi-agency working is making a significant difference to this group of children, who in previous research were shown to face barriers to being at home and accessing education.
- The professionals interviewed for the research were extremely positive about the process and outcomes of multi-agency working for them. They reported improvements to the quality of their working lives and to their relationships with other professionals, agencies and families.
- Two thirds of the 25 families included in this study reported that the multi-agency service had made a positive difference to their lives. There was some evidence that having a keyworker had a beneficial impact on families' access to services and their perception of overall quality of life. However, many families reported that social and emotional issues, as well as some practical issues around funding and equipment, were still enormously problematic.
- Many of the 18 children who took part in the study were still experiencing multiple barriers to exercising some basic human rights. These included areas of their lives such as communication, independence, friendships, relationships, leisure and recreational activities.

- Overall, the six services had worked hard to put in place structures to facilitate the process of multi-agency working. Less attention had been paid to the outcomes of multi-agency working for disabled children and their families.

Introduction

Almost 30 years of research has consistently shown that families with disabled children would prefer the many agencies that they encounter to work together more effectively. Since 1997, a strong policy emphasis on the importance of *joined-up* working has promoted the benefits of partnerships. In response, many projects and services have been established throughout the UK, which aim to implement better joint work while improving quality of life for this group of children and their families. There is, however, a notable lack of information about the nature of multi-agency services for children with complex health care needs, and, more crucially, the impact that these partnerships have on families and children.

About the study

The research outlined was the culmination of a research project conducted by a research team from the Norah Fry Research Centre at the University of Bristol and the Family Fund. The study took place between 2000 and 2003 and was funded by the Community Fund.

The project aimed to explore the experience of multi-agency working for:

- disabled children with complex health care needs;
- their families; and
- the professionals who support them.

To achieve this the research was divided into three parts:

1. an exploratory phase to determine the extent of multi-agency working for disabled children with complex health care needs in the UK;
2. visits to 26 services to collect data about their work;
3. case-study visits involving six of the services across the UK (3 in England; 1 in Wales; 1 in Scotland; and 1 in Northern Ireland). At each service, interviews were conducted with professionals (115 in total), families (25) and children/young people (18) involved in the multi-agency service.

The six services: different types of multi-agency working in services to disabled children with complex health care needs

Each service had a different model for working with families and had approached the development and provision of its multi-agency services in a range of ways. For example, each of the services had different arrangements for defining and organising the resources needed to work together. In five of the six services, one sole agency was taking a lead role (at strategic level), in terms of funding or management. At an operational level, partnerships were fulfilled by financial contributions to care packages for individual children and/or by staff from different agencies donating a proportion of their time to the multi-agency service. Only one of the six sites had established a truly multi-agency approach to resource sharing at both strategic and operational level.

The nature of services provided to families included coordinating administration and/or services and support, and providing services and support. All of the six sites were acting as points of coordination for administration or indirect elements of care provision. In addition, four of the sites were also trying to coordinate the actual services and support offered to families through the provision of a named person (known variously as a keyworker, link worker or service coordinator).

There were different levels of understanding and commitment to the aims of each of the multi-agency services. Across all the sites there was little evidence of Black and minority ethnic families accessing the multi-agency services.

The impact of multi-agency working on professionals and agencies

Working with families as part of a multi-agency team was said by professionals to be enjoyable and rewarding. They said that they had better relationships with parents and could be more effective in supporting them. Working in multi-agency services provided professionals with enhanced opportunities for personal and professional development. Staff said that they had greater insight into the work cultures of other agencies and felt enabled to look jointly at common issues.

Professionals involved in joint work reported clearer and more efficient channels of communication. However, some problems remained, due to different statutory frameworks, incompatible IT systems, and a lack of commitment from some agencies and individuals.

Overall, professionals were almost unanimous in their belief that the multi-agency services they worked in were making a positive difference to the lives of families. However, relationships between staff and families were problematic in the areas of advocacy and scarce/limited resources.

The impact of multi-agency working on families

Multi-agency services appeared to be providing effective, focused support to families in terms of managing their children's complex health care needs at home. These health needs were largely well met. Nearly two thirds of the families we interviewed reported that the multi-agency service had made a positive difference to the overall quality of their lives. However, many of the families had difficulties with daily routines, particularly sleeping.

Of those children who were of school age, all were attending a local school or nursery on a regular basis, and families expressed a high degree of satisfaction with the support and educational input their children received.

Very few families had received a coordinated response from the multi-agency service in relation to physically adapting their homes, even where there was evidence of access to a named person or coordinator.

Three quarters of the families we interviewed had a gross family income that was below the national average. General help from multi-agency services with financial management was often absent.

The families we interviewed all experienced major difficulties in finding and organising social activities for themselves and for their disabled children. The shortage of flexible, adequate and appropriate sitting or short-breaks services was thought to be responsible for this. Most families had a very strong desire to do things together and to be perceived as a whole family. Multi-agency services did not appear to be able to respond to this and the focus of support was very much on the disabled child with complex health care needs, to the detriment of the family unit as a whole.

Families reported numerous sources of emotional pressure, some of which were directly related to a lack of coordinated and flexible support from the multi-agency services. A large proportion of families felt they had no one outside the immediate family unit to turn to for emotional support. However, nearly half of the families we spoke to felt confident that they could get support from the multi-agency service if they so wished and where this was offered it was highly valued by families. Children with complex health care needs were not given access to emotional support, despite a need for this being apparent.

Over half of the families we interviewed had access to a named person, or keyworker, with a specific remit to coordinate services for them. Despite this, there was a distinct lack of clarity regarding the role of this person, and only six out of 25 families felt that the keyworker or multi-agency service did actually coordinate services for them. Many of the families we interviewed were still experiencing multiple assessments and reviews. Families did not appear to have access to regular reviews of their needs or to have a clear picture of their entitlements.

The views of disabled children and young people with complex health care needs

The vast majority of children and young people we spent time with had close, but extremely dependent, relationships with their parents or carers. Very few children could spend time alone with friends, or begin to develop some independence away from close family members.

The children and young people we spent time with had limited opportunities for developing friendships and relationships, although children with verbal communication were more likely to have significant friendships, underlining the importance of support for communication. It was also clear that this group of young people wanted to do the sorts of *ordinary* things that all children do, not necessarily activities that were *specially designed* for them.

There was little evidence of effective consultation between the multi-agency services and disabled children with complex health care needs about their care and support. Even where families had access to a keyworker, we did not get a strong sense that there were many primary relationships between this person and the children themselves. Some children were unaware of the identity of their keyworker even when named and described.

Multi-agency working for disabled children with complex health care needs and their families – has it made a difference?

In a relatively short time-span, the multi-agency services that were part of this study had brought about significant changes for families and children in terms of better support for children's complex health care needs at home and improved access to education. What appeared to be missing, however, was a wider appreciation of what still needs to be achieved in terms of social and emotional support for families, and in terms of facilitating some basic human rights for children and young people. The project team recommends that multi-agency services build upon their important work on the structure and process of multi-agency working, and develop an increased appreciation of impact and outcomes for families.

Introduction

This report explores the process and impact of multi-agency working in services to disabled children with complex health care needs. The material presented in the report is the culmination of a research project conducted by a research team from the Norah Fry Research Centre at the University of Bristol and the Family Fund. The research took place between 2000 and 2003 and was funded by the Community Fund as part of its health and social research programme.

The report is divided into seven chapters. Chapter 1 sets the scene with reference to background literature, policy and methodology. Chapter 2 provides an overview of the organisation and management of the six multi-agency services included in this research. Chapter 3 focuses on the impact of multi-agency working on professionals and agencies. Families' accounts are described in Chapters 4 and 5, both in regard to the impact of multi-agency working on daily family life and the contact that families have with services and professionals. Chapter 6 describes the experiences of children and young people with complex health care needs in regard to their well-being and their contact with professionals. Finally, Chapter 7 summarises issues relating to the process and impact of multi-agency working in services for disabled children with complex health care needs and makes recommendations for those involved in the policy and practice of multi-agency working.

All names and details of people, places and organisations have been changed to protect anonymity.

Who is the report for?

This report is aimed at practitioners, managers and policy makers working, or wishing to work, in a multi-agency way to provide services to children and families. Although the primary audience is likely to be those working to support disabled children with complex health care needs and their families, the report will also have appeal to those interested in partnership working in a wider sense, including multi-agency working between other professionals working with more diverse groups of service users. The emphasis in the report on exploring the process *and* impact of multi-agency working has wide applicability for many service sectors. The report will be of particular interest to those who are involved in setting up integrated 'Children's Trusts', in the light of the English government's recent Green Paper on safeguarding children (DfES, 2003).

Introduction to the research: why ask about multi-agency working in services to disabled children with complex health care needs?

Increasing numbers of disabled children require support for complex health care needs, often necessitating the use of medical technology at home. This group of children need support that routinely crosses agency and professional boundaries. Research consistently shows that families with such a child would prefer the many agencies that they encounter to work together more effectively (JRF, 1999; Mukherjee et al, 1999; Noyes, 1999a; Tozer, 1999). Since 1997, a strong policy emphasis on the importance of *joined-up* working has promoted the benefits of partnerships. In response, many projects and services have been established throughout the UK that aim to implement better joint work while improving quality of life for this group of children and their families.

There is, however, a notable lack of information about the extent and nature of multi-agency

initiatives for children with complex health care needs. Which agencies are involved? What nature of service is provided? And, more crucially, is multi-agency working delivering outcomes that families and children really want?

This introductory chapter synthesises relevant literature and other documentary sources in order to provide a context for the research findings that follow. (For a more detailed review of the literature in this field, particularly in relation to children with complex health care needs and their families, see Watson et al, 2002). Information about the research participants and about the methods used to collect and analyse data is also included in this chapter.

In order to place this research in context, a *pen picture* of a child with complex health care needs follows:

Sarah is six years old and lives with her grandmother. She has Infantile Batten's Disease and epilepsy. Her mother was 17 years old when she was born, and found it difficult to cope alone. She visits Sarah regularly, and has her to stay for one night a month. Sarah has had periods of being extremely unwell, and at one stage weighed only 11kg. She is mentally alert, but has no verbal communication. She is fed by naso-gastric tube, and also needs suction and oxygen therapy. She is on a wide range of drugs and also needs particular attention paid to her mouth. Her urine output needs monitoring and she also needs help with her bowels. Sarah has a wide support network, consisting of:

- Community nurses – bathing
- GP
- Consultant
- Social worker
- Care assistant – 3 sessions per week (social services)

- Nurse – 12 hours per week
- Charitable organisation
- Neighbours
- Family

continued overleaf

Sarah attends a special school when she is well enough, and has one-to-one support while she is there. The school could not find an appropriately trained escort for Sarah, so her grandmother goes with her on the school transport in the morning and a family friend goes with her in the afternoon. Sarah has a 'keyworker' who acts as a point of contact and helps find the right support and services for Sarah and her family. Sarah's grandmother and her coordinator are currently trying to persuade the education department to train and pay the family friend to be Sarah's escort.

Sarah has a particular friend called Tom at school, but he is unable to visit Sarah at home because he lives in the neighbouring town, and goes home on a different school bus.

Sarah contracted the MRSA bug while she was last in hospital, so can no longer go swimming with the school which she is very upset about. Her mother comes over once a week and takes her to a local Brownie group, which she really enjoys.

Sarah has only met her keyworker twice, once in school and once at home, but she can point to her photograph. The keyworker is her social worker and at the last review meeting it was agreed that she would try to find a suitable family so that Sarah could have short breaks, as the grandmother is finding it increasingly stressful to look after Sarah. She is beginning to have back problems, and it was recognised that she needs more help.

Services and support to children with complex health care needs and their families

Since the early 1990s, research findings have consistently emphasised that disabled children and their families need focused and coordinated support in the following areas relating to quality of life:

- *daily family life* – meal-times, sleep, travel, household chores, providing care, managing disabled children's health care needs at home;
- *physical environment* – accessibility of housing, outdoor space and local community buildings;
- *financial well-being* – sources of income (job, benefits), money management;
- *social well-being* – leisure, holidays, relationships, social support;
- *emotional well-being* – awareness of sources of family pressure, stress management, sense of control;
- *skills and learning* – access by child and family to school, college and other sources of personal development;
- *contact with services and professionals* – access to services, communicating with professionals, coordination of services and professionals.

For some families, certain areas will be more, or less, significant than others. There is no doubt that every individual, and family, has a different experience of

life, and will interpret the meaning of *quality of life* in a different way. However, in their analysis of the responses of 3,000 families of disabled children, researchers from the Beach Center in the US (Turnbull et al, 2000) found that families experience the highest quality of life when:

- their primary needs are met;
- they believe their current life situation is close to how they want it to be;
- each family member has the opportunity to pursue and achieve the goals that are important to their happiness and fulfilment.

Children with complex health care needs and their families have the same range of needs for services and support as other disabled children. But they also have additional care needs specifically related to the use of the medical technology itself. This group of children typically require technical and/or medical equipment in the home, both because of their need for intensive ongoing care, and to compensate for the loss of a vital bodily function such as the ability to breathe or feed independently (Wagner et al, 1988). Common medical technologies that are now used at home or in the community include: parenteral nutrition, enteral nutrition (for example gastrostomy), intravenous drug therapy, peritoneal/haemodialysis, oxygen therapy, tracheotomy, mechanical ventilation, cardiorespiratory monitoring, urostomy, colostomy, ileostomy and urethral catheterisation (Glendinning et al, 1999).

Disabled children with complex health care needs routinely receive support from numerous sources. The combination of this group of children's needs for health, social care and education means that it is inevitable that several agencies will be involved throughout their lives. Research has shown that, on average, families of disabled children have contact with at least 10 different professionals, and, over the course of a year, attend at least 20 appointments at hospitals and clinics (Care Co-ordination Network UK, 2001). For families of disabled children with complex health care needs, these numbers are likely to be very much higher. It is well established that the range, diversity and different levels of support are, in themselves, major problems for families (Sloper and Turner, 1992; Kirk and Glendinning, 1999; Townsley and Robinson, 2000). The sheer number of professionals who may be involved in supporting a disabled child in the community can often lead to a lack of continuity and coordination and may leave families uncertain about who to contact regarding specific problems (Wilcock et al, 1991; Kirk and Glendinning, 1999; Townsley and Robinson, 2000).

Recent research points towards the need for improved coordination and communication, both between professionals themselves, and between professionals and families. Despite this, there are many examples of poor communication between Health, Social Care and Education, and services and support for children with complex health care needs are poorly coordinated at most levels (Townsley and Robinson, 1999). This very often results in families taking on the role of keyworkers, placing a huge additional burden on them (Kirk and Glendinning, 1999). There is an urgent need for professionals and services to work together, or engage in multi-agency working, in order to improve the quality and effectiveness of support to this growing group.

Multi-agency working – the policy imperative

Multi-agency working became a policy imperative when the New Labour government fixed on *partnerships* as an alternative ethos to the internal market and competition in services (Alexander and Macdonald, 2001). Current legislation requires professionals to find ways to move across the boundaries between Health, Education and Social

Care. The concept of joint working underpins many recent policy documents and several White Papers (DoH, 1997, 2001; Cabinet Office, 1999).

Partnership in action (DoH, 1998) promoted the ideas of pooled budgets between agencies, jointly run services and lead commissioners. It proposed that these newly introduced *flexibilities* would make it easier for local authorities and health authorities to work together *at the boundaries* between health, social care, education, housing and other services.

Working in partnership is a key mechanism for delivery of services to children at risk of poverty and social exclusion in England through the Sure Start and Children's Fund initiatives. It is also prioritised in the forthcoming National Service Frameworks for Disabled Children in England and in Wales, with an emphasis on keyworking as a means of coordinating support to families. In addition, the 2003 Green Paper *Every child matters* (DES, 2003) has proposed major changes to Health, Education and Social Services with a focus on improving and safeguarding the well-being of *vulnerable children* and their families. The proposals include the creation of Children's Trusts, which will integrate key services for children and young people such as Education, Social Services, Health, Connexions and Youth Offending teams. The Green Paper also proposes legislation for introducing a lead professional, or keyworker, where children are known to more than one agency.

In Scotland, Wales and Northern Ireland, respective legislation has also highlighted the need for multi-disciplinary teams (1989 Children Act England and Wales; 1995 Children [Northern Ireland] Order; 1995 Children [Scotland] Act) and inter-agency working in services to disabled children.

Defining multi-agency working

There are many difficulties inherent in finding a term to describe how professionals and agencies work together (Leathard, 1994; Lacey and Ouvry, 2000). Terms such as 'partnership working', 'working together', 'joint working', and 'multi-agency working' are used interchangeably to explain the relationships between professionals and agencies, the way they actually work together or operationalise these relationships (Lloyd et al, 2001), as well as the quality of the work involved.

Glendinning (2002) suggests that the term 'partnership' is infused with overtones of moral value and superiority and that the lack of consensus about its meaning makes evaluation of actual partnerships very problematic. She adds, however, that the lack of a specific definition may, in practice, be a good thing, since it enables services to design initiatives that are responsive, adaptable and which reflect local circumstances.

One of the most pragmatic definitions is given by Leeds Health Action Zone (2002), which describes a partnership as when two or more people or organisations work together towards a common aim. The Department of the Environment, Transport and the Regions' definition (DETR, 1999) expands on this by recognising that partnerships are cooperative relationships and thus proposes that a partnership is a process where two or more parties cooperate and work together.

Success factors for multi-agency working

There is a well-established body of literature that addresses the question of what makes a successful partnership (for example Hudson et al, 1997, 1999; DETR, 1999; DoH and Public Services Productivity Panel, 2000; Hague, 2000; Flint et al, 2001; Kennedy et al, 2001; Atkinson et al, 2002; Banks, 2002; Leeds Health Action Zone, 2002). Indeed, Alexander and Macdonald (2001) suggest that research on multi-agency working is not now coming up with any new findings. They argue, however, that this research is not widely known, or made available to those involved in establishing and participating in partnerships and that there is thus a need to re-emphasise what is already known about how to make partnerships work. Nevertheless, there is very little research evidence that has specifically focused on multi-agency working in services to disabled children. One notable exception is work carried out by the Social Policy Research Unit (University of York) to investigate the process and outcomes of keyworking for families with a disabled child (Mukherjee et al, 1999; Mukherjee et al, 2000).

Common themes from the literature include the following 11 success factors:

1 Explicit agreement about how the partnership will pool or share resources such as time, people and money
This includes determining what resources each partner has available for the partnerships, ensuring appropriate use of all local resources and defining the extent to which there are joint approaches to investment. There should be an acknowledgement that change needs to be resourced in its own right, particularly in terms of ensuring that there are dedicated staff to lead and manage the multi-agency process.

2 Explicit agreement to a clear, shared vision that defines the purpose of the partnership, and to common objectives for achieving that vision
These objectives should include ways of achieving outcomes that are important to those people who are the focus of the multi-agency initiative. *Commitment* to this vision and to the ethos of multi-agency working is also important, but can take time and effort to engender. Multi-agency working can be difficult and time-consuming, and it is important to be aware of the amount of energy and impetus needed to keep it going, once the initial enthusiasm has worn off. Explicit commitment from individual agencies and senior managers is essential from the outset. Commitment from operational staff is equally necessary and opportunities should be sought out to develop this. Research shows that commitment from staff at all levels of an organisation is necessary to bring about effective change.

3 A clearly defined structure, or model, to explain how the multi-agency process will operate, particularly in terms of the nature of work with children and families and the expected outcomes for them
It is helpful to formalise in writing how the process will work, and to communicate this to families and children. However complex the workings of a partnership might be *behind the scenes*, people using the service should be able to understand and to access the process easily, preferably via a single point of contact.

4 Clarification of the roles, responsibilities and contributions of the people involved in the multi-agency process

This includes identifying the skills and competencies needed to meet the objectives set by the partnership and recruiting, or seconding staff if necessary. Participation of the right people is very important. Partnerships are most successful when key staff are involved who can make a difference at policy, management and practice levels. In addition, it can be advantageous to identify, or employ, key strategic people with the specialist role of forging links between organisations.

5 Effective leadership and the existence of allies and champions at strategic and operational level within all the organisations involved

The importance of networking and alliances should be explicitly acknowledged and opportunities established for building relationships, trust and openness across agency boundaries. Communication and learning and training strategies can be instrumental in helping this to happen in an organic way. Joint training, for example, is a good way for professionals to get to know each other, and subsequent regular meetings can reinforce relationships and develop shared understanding.

6 The provision of opportunities for learning, support and supervision

Working in a multi-agency way will be a new concept for many professionals and specific training and support on the challenges and opportunities can be very beneficial. Support from managers and agencies is vital for those staff directly involved in partnership work, particularly where workloads or job descriptions are affected. Learning should be ongoing and a reflective approach fostered to enable continuous improvement as the process develops. Several authors recommend setting aside protected *time out* to concentrate on learning and teambuilding for services who are engaging in joint working with colleagues from other agencies (Mukherjee et al, 2000; Leeds Health Action Zone, 2002).

7 Clear and agreed arrangements for management and accountability

Accountability and decision making can be confused where several agencies are involved. Clear performance management arrangements and a governance structure that ensures open and active decision making should be established. It is also helpful to clarify the balance of responsibility between partners and where the responsibility rests for making final decisions about aspects of the partnership. Many partnerships instigate steering groups to perform management and decision-making functions.

8 Good communication between all those involved

This involves creating initial and ongoing opportunities for partners to get to know each other and setting up a structure for communicating within and outside the partnerships. This includes a clear means of communicating regularly with children and families. Regular, open communication can help to create a culture of trust, respect and honesty. It can also support the development of *network awareness*, whereby professionals from different agencies develop a better understanding of their respective roles and responsibilities. Common assessment tools and arrangements for shared access to records can help to avoid mis-communication between professionals themselves and between professionals and families.

9 Partnership with children and families

Service-user participation in service development, delivery and evaluation is a well-established component of 'best practice' in health and social care. But the complexities of setting up multi-agency initiatives can too often mean that partnership with families, children and young people is overlooked. It is important to keep the needs of children and families at the forefront of the multi-agency process. This will ensure that the new initiative is relevant to the changing needs of children and families and will reflect local circumstances, and cultural diversity. Families and children should be involved in the planning, development and evaluation of the service or project.

10 Regular monitoring and evaluation

Any partnership should have a means of measuring the impact of its work. Partners should be involved in setting objectives and committed to achieving them. Evaluation criteria need to measure improvements in policy, practice and service-user satisfaction. If satisfactory outcomes for families and children are not achieved, then it may be worth questioning whether formalised (and possibly resource-heavy) partnership arrangements are really necessary. It is important, however, to recognise that change can take years, not months, to achieve.

11 Clarity about timescales and future planning

Setting up multi-agency partnerships can take a lot of time. This is very often underestimated and timescales need to be realistic. Many partnerships may be time-limited, particularly in terms of targeted funding. If this is the case, then a clear plan should indicate what should happen next and how, if at all, new ways of working will be embedded into mainstream provision. Professionals, families and children should be aware of the plan and its implications for service delivery.

Benefits of multi-agency working

The literature and policy on multi-agency working places great emphasis on what are perceived as the benefits of partnerships. These include improved coordination, better exchange of information (Flint et al 2001), clearer communication mechanisms, better targeted resources, common approaches to service delivery, more effective pooling of resources, translation of policies into action, enhanced understanding by service providers of issues that affect service users, and upfront identification of needs and services (Hague, 2000). Leeds Health Action Zone (2002) simply suggests that partnerships offer access to *more* of everything, such as more resources, more impact, more efficiency, more negotiating power, more equitable services, more skills, more innovation and more benefits for disadvantaged groups.

Despite such exhortations, there appears to be a dearth of evidence to support the notion that multi-agency working in practice brings about actual benefits for children and families. Snell (2003) points out that a lot of effort goes into setting up the process, but those involved can lose sight of whether multi-agency teams are delivering what clients really want. Brown et al's (2000) study found that the delivery of services to older people through *integrated* health and social care teams did not result in a greater proportion of older people living independently in their community. Moreover, the *integrated* group scored lower on quality of life indicators and were more depressed than those receiving services via *traditional* routes. Glendinning (2002) rightly points

out that the benefits to those using services still need to be clearly established in a culture where partnership working is highly valued.

Evaluating the impact and outcomes of multi-agency working

The lack of evidence on benefits for people who use services is matched by a distinct gap in the research when it comes to looking at *impact* and *outcomes* of multi-agency working. Wray et al (2001) reviewed 235 papers on multi-agency working between health and other agencies, and concluded that the focus of the studies was mainly impact on professionals, and that very minimal evidence existed in relation to impact on patients and patient care. Similarly, Hague (2000) states that within the field of domestic violence, there is almost no work on the cost-effectiveness of multi-agency working, and no clear evidence that services are improved as a result of partnership arrangements.

Banks (2002) points out that although tools exist for assessing the process of multi-agency working, tools for assessing outcomes are less developed. Glendinning (2002) discusses the inherent problems that face those attempting to evaluate partnerships. These include: difficulties in generalising from individual case studies; diverse views of different stakeholders as to what counts as success; the length of time needed to evaluate change; and causality and attribution.

Aims and methods of the research

The project aimed to explore the experience of multi-agency working for:

- disabled children with complex health care needs;
- their families; and
- the professionals who support them.

To achieve this aim, the research was divided into three parts.

Part one – exploratory phase

The exploratory phase consisted of a literature search and a scoping exercise. The scoping exercise involved mailing out a request for information to over 700 contacts across health, education, social care and voluntary sectors. Using additional networks, contacts, the Internet and other published materials, we developed a list of 95 UK initiatives where it appeared that there was some multi-agency work in progress for children with complex health care needs.

Part two – personal visits

We developed a set of criteria for assessing the services in terms of their relevance for inclusion in the research. The assessment criteria included:

- whether the service aimed, specifically, to work with children with complex health care needs and their families, and if not, the number of children with complex health care needs who were involved in the multi-agency process;
- the age of children receiving a service from the multi-agency service;
- the originating agency;
- the number of agencies involved;
- the nature of funding;
- existence of family involvement in the development and delivery of the multi-agency service;
- whether there was a single access point for families (for example via a keyworker, link worker, or coordinator); and
- whether multi-agency assessments and reviews were conducted.

We then conducted a series of personal visits to 26 services across the UK, which covered the four countries (14 in England; 4 in Wales; 4 in Scotland; and 4 in Northern Ireland) and also included a mix of urban/rural services and areas with a significant Black and minority ethnic population. The personal visits generated quantitative and qualitative data in relation to the extent and nature of multi-agency working for children with complex health care needs. Our analysis of this data allowed us to identify a secondary list of six services for inclusion in part three.

Part three – case-study visits

Part three of the research involved more in-depth collection of qualitative data in six geographically dispersed services across the UK (3 sites in England; 1 site in Wales; 1 site in Scotland; and 1 site in Northern Ireland).

At each service, semi-structured interviews were conducted with professionals, families and children/young people involved in the multi-agency initiative. Some interviews with professionals were conducted in small groups while others were conducted individually. We undertook a total of 115 interviews with a range of professionals (see Table 1), 25 interviews with families, and spent time with 18 young disabled people with complex health care needs.

The format of the site visits involved identifying a key contact person and asking them to provide us with contact details of the relevant professionals involved in the multi-agency initiative. Interviews with professionals covered their experiences of working as part of the multi-agency services; the work that the service did to support children with complex health care needs and their families; the positive and more challenging aspects of multi-agency working; and working in collaboration with professionals from other disciplines.

We did not contact families directly, but asked the key contact to forward letters, consent forms and project information to families (with a child with complex health care needs) on our behalf. We only contacted those families and children/young people who returned a signed consent form and chose to give us their contact information. Although this approach provided maximum confidentiality, it meant that once letters had been handed over to the key contact, we had no control over the sampling. Consequently we sample by age of children (see Table 2), type of medical technology (see Table 3), income status of family (see Table 4), ethnic identity (see Table 6) or parental status (see Table 6).

Interviews with families covered their contact with the multi-agency initiative and the impact of the service on their quality of life. The sessions with children and young people covered their experiences of home life, school and overall satisfaction with quality of life. For more information about the process of spending time with children please see Chapter 6.

We offered a reflection and feedback session to professionals to check out initial findings, and to feed these back to participants, in the spirit of getting research into practice as quickly as possible. For one site, this process was replaced by feedback via an interim report, and a meeting with the project manager.

All information was treated as confidential and was stored in accordance with the Data Protection Act. We provided families with a summary card explaining their rights under the Data Protection Act. All participants were promised anonymity in subsequent publications and other research outputs.

Table 1: Numbers/types of professionals interviewed

Agency type	Professional groups	Numbers of professionals interviewed
Health	Speech and language therapists	5
	Community nurses	12
	Health visitors	9
	Physiotherapists	4
	Occupational therapists	5
	Hospital nurses	1
	Psychologists	1
	Hospital consultants	6
	Operational managers	14
	Senior/strategic managers	3
	Total	60
Social care	Social workers	9
	Short breaks workers	2
	Operational managers	8
	Senior/strategic managers	4
	Administrative staff	3
	Early years intervention worker	1
	Project worker	1
	Community-based care workers	6
	Occupational therapist	1
	Total	35
Education	Educational psychologist	4
	Specialist teacher	1
	Senior educational officer	1
	Portage worker	1
	Operational manager	5
	Senior/strategic manager	2
	Nursery nurse	1
	Total	15
Voluntary sector	Operational manager	3
	Senior practitioner	1
	Advisor	1
	Total	5
	Overall total of professionals interviewed	115

Table 2: Age groups of children and young people whose families were interviewed

Age group	Number of children
0 to 3 years	4
4 to 7 years	12
8 to 11 years	7
12 to 15 years	2
Over 16	0

Table 3: The children and young people – type of medical technology used

Type of medical technology	Number of children
Enteral nutrition	22
Suction	11
Cardiorespiratory monitoring	5
Ventilation	3
Oxygen	6
Catheter	1
Humidifier	1
Nebuliser	2

Note: Numbers add up to more than 25 as some children used more than one form of medical technology.

Table 4: Income status of families interviewed

Gross family income (including benefits)	Number of families
£5,000–£9,999	5
£10,000–£14,999	7
£15,000–£19,999	2
£20,000–£24,999	4
£25,000–£34,999	2
£35,000–£49,999	3
£50,000–£74,999	0
£75,000–£99,999	1
Missing data	1

Table 5: Ethnic identities of families and children interviewed

Ethnic identity	Families interviewed	Children we spent time with
White British	23	15
White Irish	1	1
Other white background		2 (Welsh)
Chinese	1	
Total	25	18

Table 6: Parental status of families

Mother	Number
Natural	20
Adoptive	1
Grandmother	2
Foster	2

Father	Number
Natural	16
None living at home	6
Grandfather	2
Foster	1

Data analysis

The material we collected comprised the following:

- *from professionals*: semi-structured interview data in note form and on audiotape, collected via a semi-structured topic guide. This was subsequently transcribed, or summarised from the notes or by listening to the tapes. Other relevant documents, including policies, guidance, training materials and so on;
- *from families*: structured interview data in note form, collected via a structured interview schedule;

- *from children/young people*: semi-structured interview, or observational data, collected via a topic guide, and summarised in drawings or note form.

All three sources of data were analysed following established qualitative analysis procedures (Taylor and Bogdan, 1984). This involved reading and rereading the transcripts of field notes to identify major themes or issues for professionals, families and children. Using a constant comparative approach (Glaser and Strauss, 1967), emerging themes and issues were compared for similarities or differences and then grouped into broader categories.

Once the main themes had been drawn from the data, we sought to further interrogate the material in two ways. First, we examined the data with reference to a set of definitional components of multi-agency working, developed from the review of the literature and summarised under subheadings 'Defining multi-agency working' and 'Success factors for multi-agency working' cited earlier. This enabled us to describe the *process* of multi-agency working and consider its impact on professionals and their organisations. The findings from this part of the analysis are addressed in Chapters 2 and 3.

Second, we examined the data in terms of what evidence it provided about the *impact* of multi-agency working on disabled children with complex health care needs and their families. Using the factors listed under subheading 'Services and support to children with complex health care needs and their families' earlier in this chapter, we considered what difference multi-agency working was really making to the quality of life of families and children. Chapters 4, 5 and 6 describe the main findings emanating from this part of the analysis.

Summary

- *The need for multi-agency working* – disabled children with complex health care needs require support that routinely crosses agency and professionals boundaries. Many multi-agency services have been established throughout the UK with a specific focus on improving quality of life for this group of children and their families.
- *The process of multi-agency working* – there is a well-established body of literature that addresses the question of what factors contribute to successful partnership working, but there is very little research evidence about the process of multi-agency working in services to disabled children.
- *Impact and outcomes* – there is a distinct lack of evidence about the impact and outcomes of multi-agency initiatives, which have been designed specifically to meet the needs of children and families. Despite a strong policy emphasis, there is no clear evidence to support the assumption that multi-agency working contributes to improved quality of life for those children and families who it is designed to support.

2

The six services: different types of multi-agency working

How is multi-agency working structured? What were the different types of multi-agency activity characterised in the services we visited? What services were they providing to families? How were services funded, and for how long? What were the successes and challenges? This chapter draws on the findings from our interviews with professionals and examines the nature of the multi-agency services we visited as part of the research.

Overview of the six multi-agency services

As outlined in Chapter 1, we spent time at six services across the UK. In each of these sites, a multi-agency service had been established that focused, in some way, on supporting disabled children with complex health care needs and their families. The names of the six services have been changed to A, B, C, D, E and F.

Service A was set up in September 1999 and covers a predominantly rural area, with three major centres of population. The broad aim of the service is to improve the liaison between Health, Social Services and Education staff by:

- minimising the number of appointments and review meetings for families;
- providing a structure where parents and carers have access to a named keyworker to assist them on a regular basis.

Existing members of staff across all agencies providing support to disabled children and families can volunteer to become a keyworker for up to four children. There is no additional payment for the role – it is expected that professionals will take it on in addition to their usual duties.

From September 1999 two people were working directly for the service – a full-time project manager and a half-time administrative assistant – both of whom were funded and managed by Social Services. More than 100 additional people are involved in other ways. At the time of our visit, 43 disabled children (aged from 0 to 18) and their families were linked to a named keyworker, of whom 29 were disabled children with complex health care needs.

Service B is a well-established multi-agency team of 16 professionals from a wide range of disciplines. The area covered by the service is almost wholly rural, with one medium-sized town where the service is based. The team provides and coordinates services and support to disabled children (from birth to age 19) and their families. In addition to their role as specialist workers or therapists, five members of the service act as keyworkers to children and their families. At the time of our visit, the service and its 16 staff were working with 170 disabled children and their families, of whom 14 were children with complex health care needs. The service was established in 1991.

Service C is part of an integrated community Health and Social Services trust. Geographically, the area covered by the trust is mainly rural, with one medium-sized urban pocket. The trust has seen rapid growth in the numbers of children with complex health care needs. The service was first established in

1994 to support children with complex health care needs of whom there are now 110 in the area.

The service aims to meet the needs of children and families through a multi-disciplinary discharge meeting for children leaving hospital with a complex health care intervention. The service then plans and manages the care package for each child to support them to live at home/in the community. The service is part of the wider, integrated, Health and Social Services trust, where joint working between agencies is an expectation.

Service D is based in a large, rural county and was initially set up in 1999 as a three-year pilot project with Health Action Zone funding. The service now receives tripartite funding from Health, Education and Social Services.

The aim of the service was to establish a system of care coordination for children with complex needs, aged 0 to 5 years. This was achieved through establishing a multi-agency steering group, a single assessment and care plan tool, and access to link workers who act as a first/single point of contact for families, take each child and family through the assessment process, and provide ongoing coordination of services. The expectation is that every child and family will have access to a link worker to coordinate their services and support.

Two people work directly for the service – a full-time project manager and a full-time secretary – both of whom are managed by Education. More than 60 other people are involved in the service in other ways. At the time of our visit, 70 children with complex needs were being supported by the service, of whom seven were disabled children with complex health care needs.

Service E is made up of four different locality teams and was established in 1998. The area is a large, rural county, with four medium-sized towns and one significant urban area. Each multi-disciplinary team meets monthly and encompasses professionals from all key agencies. The remit of the service is to act as a central point of contact and access for children and families. Each child and family is linked with a named keyworker, who reports to one of the four teams.

A part-time project manager oversees the running of the service, and ensures that they are chaired and minuted effectively. Her time allocation for this role is minimal (20%) and is funded by Health as a component of her main job as Head of Speech and Language Therapy. Approximately 50 other people are involved in the teams as members, keyworkers, or in other ways. At the time of our visit, 226 children aged from birth to 18 were registered with the locality teams, of whom 14 were disabled children with complex health care needs.

Service F acts as a central pivot for children with complex needs who require continuing care. Thirty children are currently supported by the service, 24 of whom are disabled children with complex health care needs. The aim is to make transition from hospital to home as smooth and coordinated as possible. The service is responsible for organising and coordinating care packages for children. This involves putting together jointly funded care packages in collaboration with other agencies whereby one or more paid carers provide all the direct, physical care that a child needs, and social and emotional support for child and family.

A continuing care coordinator and two carer support nurses provide support and training to the 19 carers who are currently employed through the service. The team also puts families in touch with a keyworker in another agency who acts as the first point of contact. The service was set up in 1996 as a two-year trial project. It is now well established and the core team of three people are funded and managed by Health. Based at a hospital, the service covers a large urban conurbation including four local authority areas.

Funding arrangements and shared resources

Each of the multi-agency services had different arrangements for funding the service and for organising the resources needed to work together. The nature of these arrangements was defined in terms of which agencies were contributing what resources (money, people, buildings, and so on) at either strategic or operational level.

In all but one of the multi-agency services we visited, one sole agency appeared to be taking a lead role at strategic level. This was either in terms of funding or management of a key component of the service. The multi-agency services provided in three sites were all mainly funded, or managed, by Health. Service A's main funding contribution and management input was from Social Services. And although the service manager for service D was tripartite funded by Health, Education and Social Services, she was managed by Education and had her office base in the local education authority's (LEA) building.

At an operational level, partnerships between agencies were fulfilled by financial contributions to care packages for individual children, and/or by staff from different agencies *donating* a proportion of their time to the multi-agency service. Only one of the services we visited had managed to establish a truly multi-agency approach to resource sharing at both strategic and operational level. The manager of this service admitted that the service was funded through a combination of 'very creative and complex arrangements'. The range of posts represented on the multi-agency team was funded by Health, Social Services, Education, voluntary agencies and through specific initiatives such as Sure Start, Children First and the Carers' Strategy. In addition, the building where the service was based was owned by a voluntary organisation. The transdisciplinary nature of the service meant that staff were able to provide care packages for children that were funded, in the main, from the services budget, since the majority of input came from members of the team themselves.

Three of the multi-agency services were funded permanently, and as such were perceived as established services in their own right. The remaining three had all been funded initially on a pilot project basis, and had a more uncertain future long term. Service E was the most poorly funded of all the multi-agency services we visited. Indeed the service itself received no substantive funding; it had been established and was continuing to run on the basis of a 20% seconded (but un-funded) time input by the Head of Speech and Language Therapy who acted as coordinator. Even the administrative time and costs were *borrowed* from an existing, mainstream Health budget.

Only one service believed that the levels of funding they received were adequate to run the multi-agency service itself, and to provide the level of support required by families and children with complex health care needs in their area. Service A needed more resources for administrative support, while as noted above, service E received no ring-fenced funding whatsoever to support the overall running of the multi-agency service.

Across all the sites, the main challenges to successful resource sharing were characterised by poor funding input from Education at a strategic level, and by the reticence of several agencies, including Education, to contribute resources at operational level. There was a strong sense that Education was *missing from the picture* across all the sites we visited. Even at service B, Education's financial contribution to the service was a fraction of that committed by other agencies. In service D, a significant number of health professionals had refused to contribute their time to the service, despite a commitment at senior level from their agency. And in service E, the coordinator had experienced huge problems in ensuring appropriate representation from Education at Locality Team meetings.

Equally, however, professionals and agencies had overcome these and other challenges to successful resource sharing arrangements in a number of formal and informal ways. The need for clear and well-documented agreements for funding arrangements was referred to by several sites. The project manager at service F described a situation where, up until recently, funding for children's care packages had been agreed on a clearly documented and negotiated basis, with Health contributing 50% of the funding alongside one other agency. For example, if a child needed support to attend school, then Health and Education would each contribute 50% to cover the costs of training and employing a carer. Likewise, if a family needed a short-break service, then Health and Social Services would fund the carer on a 50/50 basis.

However, such arrangements can come under threat when new managers are appointed, who are not in tune with previously agreed funding arrangements and take the view that funding of some support packages should be the responsibility of Health alone. This highlights the need for regular and ongoing communication and the importance of keeping formal arrangements continuous and up to date.

Support from senior management was an issue highlighted by almost all of the sites. This was particularly important at the early stage of partnership development where agreements were being made about the level and nature of resources to be committed. It was also important, however, when decisions about resources for individual care packages were up for discussion. At one service, the manager found it helpful 'to take somebody more senior' to meetings where this issue was on the agenda, both to act as a champion for multi-agency input, and to ensure that a swift decision about committing resources could be made.

Clarity about roles and expectations in terms of commitment to the partnership arrangement by agencies was also important. Several sites described situations where, operationally, resource sharing was effective due to the commitment of individual practitioners, rather than the result of commitment from their managers or indeed the agency as a whole. As one senior manager put it:

> "Everyone is very committed until you start to talk about funding."

None of the sites we visited had found a way to pool mainstream budgets. One site, however, had tried on two occasions to apply for Health Act flexibilities funding, but had been told that allocation had already been identified. Another three sites were considering using Health Act flexibilities as a way to move towards pooled budgets, but all of these areas were in the midst of wider service restructuring, which they felt needed resolution before the issue of pooled budget was to be tackled. As an integrated health and social services trust, Service C received a pooled grant from the Northern Ireland Health Board. However, on receipt, this grant did not remain pooled, but was reallocated to each separate side of the agency. A pooled budget had been established for children with complex health care needs, but it was recognised that this was woefully inadequate and that, as stated above, its paucity left the service open to the possibility of legal challenges from parents.

The lack of pooled budgets in the services may serve to undermine the important task of securing

commitment from a wider range of senior managers and policy makers. Davey and Henwood (2003) make a strong connection between securing long-term funding strategies for partnership work and effectively convincing those with power to *sign up* and invest in the multi-agency agenda:

> In securing substantive rather than merely incremental change, stakeholders acknowledge the additional hurdles that lie in convincing councillors and chief executives that the investment is essential and that integrated strategies offer the only sustainable means of securing objectives. (Davey and Henwood, 2003, p 41)

Services that have used mainstream budgets under the Health Act flexibilities report a more significant impact on partnership working. Young et al (2003) looked at Welsh partnership working in social care and found that:

> The Health Act flexibilities had introduced a helpful 'nowhere to hide' attitude. Such partnerships were described as much harder edged, often replacing previous informal arrangements based on one-off opportunities and particular personalities. (Young et al, 2003, p 41)

Rationale for developing the multi-agency services

We asked respondents at each site to tell us about the history behind the multi-agency service and the rationale for its development. For three sites, multi-agency working had been developed as a direct response to commissioned research and/or a service review. In each of these sites, a previous lack of effective support for families and children was highlighted as the key motivating factor for developing a multi-agency service with specific components to meet the identified needs of this group.

For services C and F, multi-agency working had been established in response to service pressures and the demands of professionals, and was perceived primarily as a way to provide a more efficient service to families. The rapid growth in numbers of children with complex health care needs in the catchment area of service C had precipitated a clear need for designing multi-agency care packages, and establishing joint protocols and joint training for carers. At service F, the need to bring about a speedy and effective discharge from hospital was the main precipitating factor for the development of the home-based service, with perceived benefits for children, families and the service itself. A senior manager said:

> "Apart from the benefits for children and families being discharged, the initiative was also the result of pressure on paediatric intensive care beds that needed to be freed up. Parents and children were being institutionalised being in hospital for such long periods with changing staff and children not reaching their full potential."

The rationale for the development of service E was a mixture of awareness of family need (through a formal consultation process) and a response to difficulties in coordinating an effective and equitable approach to service provision across the county. The high rurality of the area, and its large geographical size, had led to very localised, and sometimes conflicting, responses to crises and difficulties, resulting in lack of equitable access to services for families. In addition, the sheer size of the area and the length of time needed for travel had caused difficulties in bringing professionals together for meetings or to provide support at home to families. The idea of Locality Teams that met regularly in four different locations across the county appeared to provide an effective solution to these problems.

It is interesting to note that of the six sites we visited, four were mainly rural and one was partly rural. It appears that for these sites the issue of rurality, and the inherent difficulties this presents in terms of communication and coordination, had been an important precipitating factor in the impetus for developing multi-agency services. In addition, despite the national policy emphasis on working in partnership, services did not refer to policy drivers as the main reason behind the development of multi-agency services (although some services had been prompted by legislation such as the 1989 Children Act). Perhaps this reflects the fact that even with a move towards increased centralisation within each of the four countries, local authorities still prefer to find local solutions to what they perceive as local problems. It may also reflect the fact that despite

providing opportunities for joint work, current legislation gives no guidance about strategies for implementing coordination.

One of the key success factors for multi-agency working (outlined in Chapter 1) is the need for explicit agreement and commitment to a clear, shared vision that defines the purpose of the partnership. If those involved in the partnership are unclear about its purpose, or indeed are uncertain that the partnership will deliver effective outcomes for children and families, then commitment to working together will be difficult to establish and maintain. Several sites paid specific attention to clarifying the rationale for joint working, and gaining commitment from the different stakeholder groups, including families. Bringing people together through one or more preliminary meetings or conferences to discuss the rationale for multi-agency working, learn more about the process and likely outcomes, and establish relationships and trust was a strategy employed by these sites. The involvement of families in these early meetings and discussions was also significant and helped to promote the benefits of multi-agency working to families themselves, while ensuring that meeting their needs was the primary focus for the development of the service. These sites had paid specific attention to the question – 'Why work in partnership?' – and had gained explicit agreement and commitment to the reasons why, in their areas, it was important for professionals and agencies to work together, and to work in partnership with families.

Aims of the multi-agency services

Respondents at each site were asked about the aims of the multi-agency services in which they were involved. Although each service had its own, sometimes quite specific, aims, some broad themes emerged.

All of the services had aims that sought to coordinate, standardise, clarify or simplify aspects of service provision for disabled children and their families. These included things like: coordinating discharge planning; setting up a system for sharing information and records; coordinating and clarifying systems and documentation for care planning, assessments and reviews; and coordinating and standardising the verbal and written advice given to families.

Four of the sites had developed a multi-agency service that aimed to ensure that families and children had access to a named person to coordinate and facilitate their care and support. For the two other sites where there was no explicit remit to provide families with a key person to coordinate services, respondents nevertheless referred to one of the aims of the service as being to act as a central pivot, or point of contact for families and children. A related aim, held by several sites was to reduce duplication of services and to minimise the number of appointments and professionals taking up the time of families.

Other aims included: to support disabled children with complex health care needs at home, thus avoiding residential placements; to raise awareness of and improve understanding of the existence and needs of this group of children; and to make better use of existing resources by working together and sharing resources more effectively.

People involved in the services

Each service had broadly the same kinds of people at the heart of planning, managing and delivering multi-agency services to families and children. These were:

- senior managers, usually at commissioner level, who had been involved in giving their agency's backing to projects in principle, and with resources;
- project managers who took the day-to-day lead on managing the operational side of the service;
- direct care/support staff from statutory and voluntary agencies (see Table 1 in Chapter 1) who worked directly with children and families.

Senior managers

Senior managers played an important role in offering support and resources to services. Their involvement usually came through their attendance at steering or management group meetings. Their presence was thought to be an important marker of the commitment of an agency to the principles of multi-agency working and partnership. Senior managers, however, were also not always clear about the details

of how services were being managed and run, and this was a source of concern to some.

Project managers

Project managers had important and often highly visible roles. They supported and encouraged professionals across agencies and acted as ambassadors for the work in a range of different arenas. Project managers had a wide range of tasks including the recruitment of volunteers, paid carers and keyworkers. They were normally responsible for coordinating and promoting training opportunities for staff and for being at the centre of promoting relationships between the different agencies that were part of the multi-agency service. It was also common for project managers to retain a small workload of direct relationships with families and children. It was clear to us that project managers in each service had extremely heavy workloads and that the process of managing the service was very demanding. The project manager in service D described a role that was broadly similar to the project managers in the other services:

> "So my main role and responsibility is to get the three statutory agencies basically working together, to agree some basic ground rules, definitions, common understandings, and then to agree a format for a single assessment and care plan tool for children with complex needs, and a process which would also include the appointment of a link worker for each child, who goes through the process. So that is my main task and responsibility and also to monitor and evaluate the success of the project."

Most, if not all, of the project managers were described to us as 'champions' of their service and of multi-agency work. Banks (2002) believes that successful partnerships rely heavily on 'network entrepreneurs' or 'champions' as we, and others (for example Mukherjee et al, 1999) have described them. In the six services we visited there were clearly individuals (often the project managers) who had worked extremely hard to push forward the multi-agency agenda, but sometimes at the price of almost unmanageable workloads and personal stress. Some of these professionals were given a certain amount of dedicated time to do this work but others were not. Banks (2002) notes that people in this role:

... are often expected to undertake both the 'day' job and the role of change management ... most are given little backing, training or time to work with new partnerships and tackle conceptual and practical problems. (Banks, 2002, p 10)

Having strong champions and allies is a prerequisite to sustaining commitment to multi-agency working, but there are obvious fragilities inherent in too few people being at the forefront of bringing about change. Concerns were expressed in the services we visited about *key* people leaving posts. This raises a question about the depth and breadth of commitment from agencies as a whole to multi-agency work. Harries et al (1999) note how common it is for services to suffer once significant professionals leave post:

... they are often highly motivated and make a difference while they are in their job but they often 'burn out' and leave. (Harries et al, 1999, p 20)

Direct care and support staff

Table 1 (in Chapter 1) illustrates the range and diversity of staff working in the six multi-agency services. In four of the six services, new job titles had been created to describe new roles for staff in the new, multi-agency context. These services had *keyworkers* as a formal part of their service. This generally meant that a named worker would act as a family's primary contact and first port of call for help and support in accessing services and professionals. Sites had different terms for this role: service coordinator, link worker, keyworker – in this report we will use the term 'keyworker' to describe this role. None of these four sites had designated keyworkers in that all of the staff taking on this role did it as part of their existing job. Of the two services not offering access to a keyworker, managers at service C said they had not been persuaded that a keyworker model was sufficiently beneficial for families. And service F did not have capacity to offer a formal keyworker scheme, although some paid staff said they sometimes informally took on this role.

Staff generally volunteered for the role of keyworker where strong pre-existing relationships with families were in place. Given that in most services families had a choice about who they wanted to act as

keyworker, it meant that some professionals did not feel that they had a real choice about whether or not to take on the role. As one person put it:

"Well I didn't really decide, it was sort of expected as part of what I was doing really.... I have to say, there was an expectation that we would. That wasn't said in so many words, but the group of children being targeted were the children that we see and at first I think you just gulped and said, 'oh no another piece of work to do'."

Service F did not operate a keyworker system, but provided packages of home-based care by employing carers to work with families. In this service the project manager was employed to pull together home-based services and act as a central point of reference so that families with children with complex health care needs could get access via the service to equipment, services and professionals.

Management

Evaluations of other multi-agency models to meet the needs of disabled children (for example Mukherjee et al, 1999; Beattie, 2000) have routinely stressed that clear and effective structures for management and decision making have a crucial impact on whether or not a multi-agency service is successful.

Management of the services overall

Each service had a clearly identifiable project manager responsible for day-to-day operational decision making in consultation with their staff team. However, given the multi-agency focus of each service, managing the service at a strategic, policy and budgetary level might be more appropriate for a multi-agency management group on which all relevant agencies and partners would be represented at an appropriate level. This was not the case in any of the six services that had different ways of structuring the management of the service. Four of the six services had similar arrangements, that is a multi-agency steering/business management group consisting of senior managers from each of the main agencies involved in the service – typically Health, Education and Social Services. The project manager who was accountable to her manager in health effectively managed one service. The other service had no formal structure of multi-agency management, but felt the service was managed between the two senior managers in Health and Social Services.

The most well-developed management group was in service A, where a county-wide, multi-agency management group was responsible for the overall management of the budget, and operational and strategic development of the project. It included senior managers from statutory and voluntary agencies, as well as parent representatives.

However, common to each service with a management group in place was a lack of clarity about the scope and role of the group. From our interviews with professionals, it appeared that people's understanding of the role of the management group was characterised by confusion and uncertainty, even down to the terminology used to describe the nature of the group's activities. Some people referred to it as a 'steering group', or 'advisory group', for example. Professionals were uncertain about whether management of the multi-agency service was in the hands of the management group, or the project manager. It was unclear whether the management groups were able to make decisions on their own, or whether they existed to support the project manager in their own decision making about the operational and strategic running of the service.

The composition of the management groups was an important issue. Only one group had parent representatives. One service had changed its structure so that parents were no longer involved. This was said to be because managers felt inhibited from discussing finances and decisions based on resources in front of parents.

Not every management group felt that it had the *right* membership of professionals. One group lacked members who could make decisions about resources and commit their agency's money at the meeting, which was felt to be problematic as it led to delays around decision making. Another group was composed of members at assistant director level, which the project manager felt was not appropriate as they did not have enough day-to-day responsibility for services directly relevant to disabled children.

A point commonly made was that putting structures together that facilitate multi-agency work takes time. This time input was said to be frequently underestimated:

> "... another interesting thing around decision making that I think wasn't taken account of ... is, that when they put in the bid for this project and others, they didn't allow the management time for the project, so they didn't provide any real structure about how are we as agencies to make the decisions that are needed."

Decision making and accountability

A lack of clarity about managerial structures exacerbated confusion about decision making and accountability within services. Professionals gave very conflicting accounts of who they felt was ultimately responsible for the service. Some felt that the agency that employed the project manager was responsible.

The fact that accountability was not always clear troubled only a small number of professionals we interviewed. In service F, however, the lack of clarity was perceived by one member of the service as a real obstacle to multi-agency work, and partly because of confusion about who was accountable and partly because of the possible repercussions of something going wrong and legal action ensuing:

> "This is a real issue! Lines of management for patient care are completely confused – as children move between medical and community directorates as they move from the [acute setting] to the [multi-agency service]. There's no clear plan for accountability – in a medico-legal sense, or in a more general sense as they move through the system. It makes it very difficult for us to work together as a team."

Underlying this tension is the fact that none of the services had a pooled budget and were therefore all potentially accountable to a range of different people and agencies. A manager at service B felt that the question of 'divided responsibilities' could potentially be resolved through the use of the Health Act flexibilities. This had been pursued, but the service had not been successful at the time of writing.

Arrangements for training, support and supervision

The range of skills and expertise needed to work jointly across agency boundaries for children with complex health care needs can be significant. Training is an important way of developing skills and confidence to do this. The use of inter-agency training is a good way to enable professionals to share skills and knowledge and to develop their expertise in new areas. Mukherjee et al (2000) recommend setting aside protected 'time out' to concentrate on learning, training and team building for staff and services involved in joint working with other colleagues and agencies.

The most common theme across services in relation to training was that there had not been enough opportunities for training about the specific dynamics of multi-agency working. Two aspects of this that were most frequently mentioned were training around chairing meetings and minute taking. This was especially true for those who adopted a keyworker role and would have liked more training and information about what it would entail:

> "There was no specific training about being a keyworker and at times that's been a problem but I did learn a lot on the job."

One service had offered staff training opportunities that explicitly addressed the specifics of multi-agency working. In this service and over a two-year period the project manager had organised training days for potential keyworkers. These took place over a full day and covered the following topics:

- role-play exercises to understand the experiences of families;
- the needs of families and children;
- child protection;
- the ethos behind service coordination and the background to the project;
- establishing written contracts between service coordinators and families;
- how to organise and chair a multidisciplinary meeting;
- administrative features of the project, that is forms and paperwork.

In service E, a coordinator described a two-day conference that focused on the whole ethos of the multi-agency team and which included presentations about coordinating and team working. Several families also made presentations and the event was felt to be very helpful.

Many professionals said their access to other training opportunities had widened, given their relationships with colleagues from other agencies, as they were often able to access training organised by them. At service C, managers from different disciplines had attended a day's training together on improving communication.

There was both informal and formal support available to professionals and, especially, keyworkers. Professionals were satisfied with their opportunities for supervision, which often came from the service manager. Some sites had keyworker meetings and forums for staff to meet and exchange information and experiences. The quote from a professional below sums up the benefits of attending multi-agency meetings with peers:

> "The meeting can sometimes be almost like a clinical supervision session – we can offload to other professionals. I find it quite therapeutic."

Clerical and administrative support was a significant issue across all but one of the services. Additional resources to pay for secretarial support were generally not available, leaving existing administrative staff overstretched or professionals taking on additional clerical work themselves. This was cited as a major difficulty, both in terms of the toll on individuals and the professionalism of the service:

> "It needs organisational and administrative support, not on the hoof, but in a properly coordinated and professional way with good documentation."

Communication

Good communication between all those involved in multi-agency working is an essential component of a good service. This involves communication between professionals, and between professionals and families, including children and young people.

Services provided a number of formal and informal structures, and opportunities to enable professionals to meet and talk with each other. The most commonly cited formal opportunities were at steering/management group meetings, team meetings, and meetings to assess and determine levels of support and service, as well as reviews.

Staff at service B shared a building and met regularly to discuss children. They talked about excellent communication, especially in terms of being able to draw on each other's expertise and specialisms, quickly and easily. Apart from the chance to meet at training sessions, keyworkers in service A did not have any structured opportunities to communicate with one another. However, several keyworkers said that they were able to talk to other keyworker colleagues on an informal, ad hoc basis. The project manager felt that communication between different agencies would be improved by an integrated computer system.

In service C, senior managers from the different agencies said that they met regularly and sent out joint written communications to staff to ensure both Education and Health and Social Services were kept informed and able to 'present a unified approach'.

Each service had investigated shared databases and information sharing between agencies, but with limited success. The main reasons for this were incompatible IT systems and disagreement about the legality of sharing information between agencies. Health were often said to be the most cautious agency when it came to raising confidentiality issues about sharing information, but not always. In one service, Education was perceived as putting up barriers to information sharing. The project manager was asked about agencies sharing records and said:

> "Well, no, that is something that is being worked on at the moment, they are just about to change the system, and there's all these issues that Education are throwing up about confidentiality, and it's quite intriguing that Health are being a bit more open about what can be shared, and Education are always saying, 'no, that's fine, we will take all of yours but we'll only give you so much or ours'."

In terms of communication strategies that may enhance communication between families and

professionals, only one service had developed a formal tool for sharing information between families and all the professionals that supported them. Service A had developed a *hand-held* record format for families. This involved families having a plastic wallet, which they could take with them to appointments and meetings, and which professionals would complete with them. However, there were concerns that in a short session there may not be enough time for the professional to read the records and that they would still ask for and rely on a summary account from the parents.

There was also evidence of concerted attempts to publicise the existence and work of the services by producing leaflets, posters, giving talks at parents' support groups and meetings, and writing articles for newsletters. The project manager at service B had visited all GP practices and heads of primary and secondary schools to talk about the service. Some project managers were involved in a national organisation that looks at issues around coordination. As a result there were opportunities to talk about their services at regional and national conferences.

Services provided to families

We asked professionals at each site to tell us about the nature of their work with families and the support provided by each multi-agency service. Their responses, synthesised in this section, reflect a wholly professional-based view of the services provided to families. Families' perceptions of the services provided, and the impact of multi-agency working (as characterised in each of the six sites) are outlined in Chapters 4, 5 and 6.

The nature of support provided to families by the six multi-agency services was defined in one or more of the following ways:

- coordinating administration, such as coordinating care packages, funding and/or information;
- coordinating services and support;
- providing services and support.

All of the six sites were acting as points of coordination for either administrative, or indirect, elements of care provision. This included coordinating things like discharge planning, care planning, assessments and reviews. In addition, four of the sites were also trying to coordinate the actual services and support offered to families. To achieve this, these sites had developed a multi-agency service that aimed to ensure that families and children had access to a keyworker to coordinate and facilitate their care and support.

Eligibility and referral

Three of the multi-agency services were actually providing direct care and support to children and families through a multi-agency team, or through a specific service set up with a multi-agency remit. For two services this included attempting to provide all the physical and nursing care a disabled child with complex health care needs might need during the day or night. Both these sites operated a service led by community nurses, which offered access to families to one or more paid and specially trained carers to support their child during the day and/or at night. Of all of the sites, only service B was coordinating both administration *and* services and support (through a keyworker scheme), in addition to acting as a multi-agency direct service provider.

The process of eligibility and referral to each of the multi-agency services was based on geographical limitations for all of the six sites. Due to inadequate resources, one site had also decided to further limit eligibility by offering the service only to children aged 0 to 5. Three sites had instigated eligibility criteria with the specific aim of restricting access to the service. This was in order to respond to concerns that these three services were under-resourced and could only provide support to a limited number of children and families. Four of the sites offered a service to all disabled children (including disabled children who also had complex health care needs), whereas two sites were set up with the specific aim of providing services and support only to children with complex health care needs and their families.

Two sites had specified that referral to the service was from professionals only, while four sites had an open referral system where anyone connected with the child or family (including any family member) could refer a family to the service. All sites, however, operated a referral system that was only activated by clear and documented consent from the family to

agree to an assessment of eligibility, or if that was already clarified, to an assessment of child/family need.

Single point of contact

As we saw in Chapter 1, families should be able to access multi-agency services via a single pathway, or point of contact. The provision of a keyworker in four of the sites provided a system for operationalising this process, and professionals were generally positive about the potential benefits for families. However, it remains to be seen whether the presence of named people did in fact facilitate better and easier access to multi-agency services for this group of families. In two services a lack of clarity from professionals about both the existence and relevance of a single point of access for families did not appear to correspond with the aims of these services to act as a central pivot or point of access.

Communicating information about the service to families

Chapter 1 stressed the importance of formalising in writing how the multi-agency process will work in practice, and to communicate this to families. Five of the sites had something in writing that they were able to share with families, ranging from a handbook to a short, but clear and helpful, leaflet. However, our interviews with professionals showed that even when a clearly defined statement to describe the aims and purpose of the service was available, there was still confusion and disagreement about basic issues such as eligibility criteria, referral, individuals' roles in providing a multi-agency service, nature and regularity of reviews, and so on.

Responding to diversity

The ability of a multi-agency service to respond to the changing needs of families and children, including those from Black and minority ethnic groups, is a key success factor for joint working, which aims to improve services and support for these groups. For all sites, the level and nature of input offered to each family was decided following a multidisciplinary assessment or profile of needs. It was unclear as to the extent to which services were able to offer a truly flexible and responsive approach to child and family need. Indeed, evidence from professionals appeared to indicate that despite paying lip-services to the ethos of a needs-led service, most sites were constrained by budgets, staffing levels and waiting lists in their ability to respond flexibly to the real needs of families and children. In addition, a lack of clarity in the data about the regularity and nature of reviews indicates little scope for responding to the changing needs of children and families over time.

Only one site had a significant Black and minority ethnic population. Across all sites there was little evidence of Black and minority ethnic families using the multi-agency services on offer. Two services said that they were not doing enough to include Black and minority ethnic families. In service D, a social services manager suggested that there was 'little understanding of cultural diversity' in the area.

Most professionals, when asked, said that there would be access to interpreters if a need arose. In one service, however, there was no budget to pay for any interpreting and it was suggested that clarification would be needed about who would meet the cost, should the need for this service arise. The majority of staff in each service felt that they would be able to meet the needs of minority groups. However, when we interviewed a family from a minority ethnic background it was clear that the service was not meeting their language needs. The family did not seem to know who their named person or service coordinator was, although they were seeing professionals who were trained service coordinators. They also did not attend meetings, due to finding it difficult to understand and be understood.

In service F, one professional said that the small numbers of Black and minority ethnic children using the service did not reflect the fact that there was a significant Black population in the area. However, this professional felt that there were cultural issues within the extended families that meant that they were less likely to accept short breaks as an option for their child. This is an assertion routinely challenged and contradicted by research evidence (see Beresford, 1995; Chamba et al, 1999; Flynn, 2002).

There were a number of other minority groups living in the areas covered by the services – notably Irish-, Welsh- and Chinese-speaking communities and people from the 'travelling' community. There were staff fluent in Irish and Welsh, but Chinese families were said not to have come forward for services.

Partnership with children and families in the planning and development of services

If families are real partners with professionals in multi-agency services, then we would expect to see them given opportunities to be involved in the planning, development and evaluation of the service. Professionals spoke about individual families being more involved in the planning of their own support and services, but this section deals with how much families were included in the development of the service as a whole.

Most services had carried out consultation with parents at the point at which their service was being put together. Families' experiences were said to be the impetus for multi-agency work. In one service, consultation meetings and a conference had been organised to find out from parents how they wanted the service to develop. In this service, parents were represented on the management group and as part of a separate reference group of parents. In another service, parents were asked their views (via a questionnaire) about the setting up of both the service itself and whether a new Child Development Centre would be helpful to them. A subsequent meeting, to which all parents were invited, discussed themes emanating from the questionnaire. As attendance by parents was low, individual keyworkers followed up issues informally with parents who, as a group, expressed general satisfaction with the plans for the service.

In service D the project manager had consulted with parents of children at special schools about the development of the service. At the end of the process, parents met with the project steering group to describe their experiences and concerns. Additionally, two parents had been on the recruitment panel for the appointment of the project manager.

In the other three services there was little evidence of families being formally involved in the planning, design or management of services. There was, however, a recognition by professionals at all three sites, that more work needed to be done in this area. One service felt that it had needed time to develop and 'work out what they were about' before getting parents involved. A health professional in service C had tried to recruit parents to be on a planning group, but had been unsuccessful and talked about the difficulties in doing this:

> "We've had to develop the service at a rapid pace and just about kept up with procedures and protocols. We've not had a chance to go out and talk with parents, do all the extras. Involvement is non-existent, due to lack of staff time and time pressure to provide a statutory service. It is government policy to consult but it is very difficult to get a parents group together."

There were mixed views on the feasibility or desirability of having parents on project management steering groups. A senior manager in one service, for example, accepted that a change in attitude was required in order for this to happen:

> "We would like to be able to support more parents by being involved at senior management planning stages as well. I think that it is something that we would like to ensure can happen and not be just as a token representative but as an active partner there needs to be a shift of attitude in perhaps some of the senior professionals as to how that might happen."

We did not find any examples of children and young people being involved from the outset in the planning or design of services. The project manager in service D suggested that it would be difficult to engage children and young people in a process-oriented piece of work:

> "It's very abstract, and it's about a process and that is not very interesting for young people, so I have thought quite carefully about how to involve young people, so what I did do was I did a very simple questionnaire with symbols on it for young people about their experience of assessment and what they felt about the way people talked to them and what tips they might have to offer."

Monitoring and evaluation

Finding out what difference the service is making to families from a range of perspectives is crucial. It allows for services to be shaped and developed. It provides evidence of outcomes, which can promote good practice in other settings and be used to secure future funding. Systems of monitoring and evaluation need to find out how children, families and the professionals that support them are experiencing the service.

Overall, there was little evidence of systematic monitoring and evaluation procedures built into services. Questionnaires that asked about parental satisfaction with services were commonly used. One site discussed the expectation that their service would be routinely audited, but this was not always done. Service C did routinely monitor certain performance indicators for children's services as a whole, which included the services received by children with complex health care needs.

Two services had been independently evaluated as one-off exercises by university researchers. Eight families that we interviewed told us that their opinions had been sought about the service or project, either formally via questionnaires, or at meetings, or informally, via their keyworker. There were a number of other ways in which the views of parents were sought, including celebration and *pamper* days for families, which were an opportunity for parents and professionals to get together in a social context and relax, but also feedback on how the service was doing. However, there was no clear evidence that any of the sites had fed back findings from monitoring or evaluation to families in an appropriate or accessible way.

The involvement of children and young people with complex health care needs in the services painted a less positive picture, with only two children being talked to by their coordinator and being asked their opinion about different aspects of their care.

Summary

- *Six sites* were visited as part of the research. Of these, four were mainly rural, one was partly rural, and one was wholly urban. Each site had established a multi-agency service that focused, in some way, on supporting disabled children with complex health care needs and their families. Each site had a different model for working with families and had approached the development and provision of its multi-agency services in a different way.

- *Resources* – each of the multi-agency services had different arrangements for defining and organising the resources needed to work together. Just one site had established a truly multi-agency approach to resource sharing at both strategic and operational level. Half of the sites had permanent funding, while the other half were funded on a short-term basis. Challenges to successful resource sharing had been overcome in a number of ways, including: producing and agreeing clearly written agreements for funding arrangements, and highlighting the need for senior managers to recognise the importance of shared resources, and to act as champions for funding arrangements at strategic and sometimes operational levels.

- *Impetus* – there were many reasons why multi-agency working had been adopted by each of the six sites. These included: a response to commissioned research and/or a service review; a response to service pressures and demands of professionals; a way to provide a more efficient and equitable service; awareness of family need. While some services referred to legislation as a prompt to work collaboratively, this was generally not the main impetus.

- *Aims* – aims of the multi-agency services included: to coordinate, standardise, clarify or simplify aspects of service provision; to give families and children access to a named person to coordinate and facilitate their care and support; to support disabled children at home; to raise awareness of and improve understanding of this group of children; and to make better use of resources.

- *People involved* – each multi-agency service was composed of senior managers, project managers, and direct care and support staff. Professionals looked to senior managers to be important supporters of the service and commit resources. Project managers were usually perceived as 'champions' and the people who had the closest grasp of operational and strategic issues in the service. There were a wide range of direct care and support staff acting as the main link between the service and families and children.

- *Management arrangements* – the services adopted different managerial approaches with four of the six services having management or steering groups while there were less formal structures of management in the other two services. However, common to each was a lack of clarity about the role and scope of management arrangements for the service overall. There was also uncertainty about who was ultimately accountable for the service.

- *Training and support* – professionals felt that there were insufficient opportunities for training around the specific dynamics and intricacies of working in a multi-agency team. At the same time, access to training and personal development had generally increased as a result of having access to the training provided by all of the agencies involved in the service. The lack of designated clerical and administrative support was cited as being highly problematic in all but one service.

- *Communication* – services provided both formal and informal ways for staff to communicate and share information with each other, and on the whole, professionals felt that communication was greatly improved by working in a multi-agency context. Problems around the incompatibility of IT systems and concerns about sharing databases hindered the effective sharing of records and data.

- *The nature of services provided to families* – these included coordinating administration and/or services and support, and providing services and support. All of the six sites were acting as points of coordination for administration or indirect element of care provision. In addition, four of the sites were also trying to coordinate the actual services and support offered to families through the provision of a keyworker. Just one site was coordinating both administration, and services and support (through a keyworker scheme), as well as acting as a direct service provider. There was a lack of clarity and some confusion among different professionals about various basic elements of the multi-agency services, such as eligibility criteria, the referral process, and the nature and regularity of reviews.

- *Cultural diversity* – only one site had a significant Black and minority ethnic population. Across all the sites there was little evidence of Black and minority ethnic families accessing the multi-agency services. Some services recognised that they needed to be more proactive in promoting their services to Black and minority ethnic families.

- *Consultation* – families had been consulted quite widely about the services at different stages. Involving families fully in services was seen as important by services, but this was seen as work that was sometimes difficult to do. There was little evidence of children and young people having a say in the development of services.

- *Monitoring and evaluation* – systematic and regular monitoring and evaluation was lacking in each of the services. Where it existed, monitoring and evaluation was more commonly an ad hoc activity, characterised, for example, by sporadic service audits, parental questionnaires and one-off external evaluations. Children and young people were rarely asked their views about the services they received, and feedback from monitoring and evaluation activities to either children or their families was rare.

3

The impact of multi-agency working on professionals and agencies

Multi-agency work can be challenging and time-consuming. It often requires professionals to work in new ways with a range of different individuals and organisations. While the outcomes of multi-agency working are assumed to focus on improving services for children and their families, it is also useful to consider the impact of multi-agency working on professionals, as they are key to the delivery of joined-up services.

The focus of this chapter is the impact that multi-agency work had on the professionals involved in the following areas: skills and knowledge; role and professional identity; communication; workload; relationships with other professionals; service provision; and, work and relationships with families.

Impact on skills and knowledge

Working across traditional professional boundaries can provide opportunities for staff to develop new skills and knowledge in a number of different ways. A very strong theme across sites was that professionals felt that they knew much more about each other's roles than they had before. They believed this to be the result of working more closely together in multi-agency teams, meetings and forums.

Staff said that finding out more about each other's roles and responsibilities enabled them to be more efficient in their responses to families:

"It's made me more organised about my own role, more focused. I used to go off as a loose canon – disappear off down the wrong path. Now I find out

who is able to do things and it makes things happen more quickly and saves a lot of time and energy."

In service D, a keyworker from a health background described the challenge in finding out who she needed to contact when putting together a large package of home care for a child reliant on a ventilator:

"It's been a very disjointed experience working with two trusts, each with different budgets and people and ways of doing things. It was hard to know who to even set up a meeting with. It's a big package of care and a steep learning curve."

As a result of this the site was designing 'route maps' which highlighted and clarified different professionals' roles and responsibilities.

As well as learning about each other's roles in relation to individual children and families, there were opportunities to reflect on issues that crossed disciplines. So for example, in one site, there had been multi-agency fora to discuss confidentiality and consent, which had resulted in a more consistent approach across agencies.

Multi-agency working provided welcome opportunities for professional and personal development. Professionals said that they gained knowledge about the nature and culture of other agencies as well as individuals working within them:

"Personally – it's been very good in terms of personal development. I've always felt that I was a good team player. But [the teams] have helped me to develop my knowledge of what other people do. And knowing about other departments and their strengths/ weaknesses is very useful."

Impact on role and professional identity

We wanted to know if working in multi-agency teams and/or in multi-agency services changed how professionals perceived their own roles and their sense of professional identity. Providing a more 'joined-up' service to families may require professionals to work across traditional professional boundaries and possibly to expand on their role.

Lacey and Ouvry (2000) and Doyle (1997) discuss concepts of 'role release' and 'role expansion', which they argue are key to effective collaborative working. Role release implies the transfer of skills and sharing of expertise to an individual or group. Role expansion involves training in the concepts and language of another discipline. Both these concepts involve a certain amount of trust between professionals in order that roles are released and expanded to allow people to take each other's places. This is a demanding process and professionals must first feel secure in their own roles and have confidence in their own abilities (Hart, 1991). Some professionals may find these experiences very threatening. Brown et al (2000) point out that the erosion of roles is both opportunistic and threatening.

As described in Chapter 2, four of the six services had created a new professional role of 'keyworker'. Clear guidelines on the nature of this role were not always evident. Some staff said this meant that families did not always know what to expect from them. (This was despite the fact that three of the sites had information packs for staff about the role of a keyworker.) Staff gave us different accounts of how they interpreted the role of keyworker. Some felt able and willing to take on a lot of additional tasks associated with keyworking, whereas others were more *hands off*. In service E, for example, one keyworker said that her approach was to tell families who to get in touch with themselves, rather than take on this aspect of support herself.

Ultimately, professionals developed the role of keyworker individually and in ways in which they were confident and comfortable:

"The role's a bit fuzzy but it has to be. It depends on the individual and the family. Each relationship is unique and based on an individual assessment. I have a lot of personal autonomy so I just go ahead and do what I think is right."

In three sites, some professionals said that working relationships with colleagues from other disciplines were so strong that there had been an expansion of their role. They were all prepared to take on any task within their capability, which effectively supported families rather than saying, 'I'm a social worker and I don't do that kind of task', for example:

"It's made a big difference. I can work in different ways than just a social worker would. As a social worker I would ask, 'how is this child getting on?', but now I feel we can sort out particular problems together."

Staff in this site said that they were forced to leave their specialisms behind as part of the multidisciplinary team and instead adopt a new role of keyworker, but which also drew on their own and each other's specialist knowledge:

"We see ourselves less as health visitors or social workers or whatever and more as coordinators."

"I trained as a social worker but now I think I've got a new professional identity. The boundaries are clearer."

A physiotherapist who also acted as a keyworker reflected on how the role has impacted on her sense of professional identity:

"I think we do more cross-over work now. We are more 'generic' in our roles – we will take on aspects of other people's roles and pick up things that other people might normally do. There are huge benefits for families. We don't say 'you'll have to wait for the OT to come to do this' – we just get on and deal with it ourselves. We're not precious about our professions."

One professional discussed how he had to be thoughtful about when he was working with a family with his label of *keyworker* and when he was there in his capacity as *therapist*. This professional had constructed quite clear boundaries around his different roles:

> "... it changes my role with families. It's very task orientated – fixing meetings, conflict resolution, but this inhibits my role as therapist. They see me instead as a fixer of things. We've talked about this – me and my two families and now I'm clear what hat I'm wearing when I go – link worker or psychologist and that's been good and restored my therapeutic relationship with them."

A keyworker at service B (a site where most of her colleagues discussed their positive experience of 'role blurring') was less clear about how to reconcile her professional identity and status as a social worker with her developing role as a keyworker:

> "Bit of a conflict working for social services and working for [the team]. I trained as a social worker and then come here to [the team] where it's completely different and sometimes it's difficult to reconcile the two. Sometimes it's a bit of a personal dilemma – how much I am working in the [team] way and how much am I working in the social services way?"

Senior managers spoke less about the process of role blurring and were more inclined to highlight their view that the specialist contribution made by various staff members in a team was significant. One senior manager sounded a note of caution about professionals working outside of their area of expertise. This manager felt that difficulties had arisen from 'well-intentioned people overstepping their roles'. The example given was of a non-physiotherapist suggesting at a care planning meeting that a particular child needed a walking frame:

> "This wasn't clinically appropriate for this child and the 'unpicking' took a lot of careful work."

Our research found evidence of role expansion and role blurring and most direct care and support staff were positive about the opportunities that this provided for them to work in new ways. However, one group of professionals felt unsure about their role in working with children with complex health care needs. So in four sites there was discussion about the role of social work and social services in the lives of disabled children with complex health care needs.

There were concerns about how working with children with complex health care needs meant that medical and health care issues dominated. Social workers were not always sure or confident about their role in what they perceived to be an 'overtly medical situation'.

At service A, a senior manager felt that health professionals were more likely than social workers to form strong relationships with families because "the needs around these children are medical-based". Indeed, social workers in one service gave a despondent account of their role with children with complex health care needs and their families. They said that they lacked experience of working with children with complex health care needs and felt that there was a dominance of medical professionals. They described poor working relationships and expected parents to see them as:

> "... gatekeepers who work within a non-responsive and outrageously bureaucratic system."

One social worker questioned the role of keyworkers with generic tendencies and felt that social workers should automatically be keyworking for families whether or not the work had a formal title:

> "If I was doing my job properly I'd be looking at the needs of a child and family holistically and then coordinating things for them. So what does a coordinator do? I don't have the experience of being rung up by a coordinator who says, 'I'm the coordinator and I need to sort out a, b, c'. I don't see any noticeable difference if a family does have a coordinator. At the end of the day you can't reduce the range of professionals that a family need to see – you can't cut out the physio."

At the same time some health professionals questioned the value of the social work role. In one service, a health professional said she felt that social workers had a *privileged position*, standing slightly outside of things while health professionals get on with the 'nitty-gritty of day-to-day care', which also inevitably meant that they responded to parents' emotional needs as well.

Later in this report there will be discussion about the relationship and balance struck between meeting the health needs and the other social and emotional needs of children and their families. It is interesting that some social workers felt that a 'social model of disability' was being threatened by the dominance of medical and health issues. Revans (2003) writes that the 'blurring of boundaries' synonymous with joint working between health and social services does contribute to the erosion of the social model of care as social workers' independence diminishes:

> Social workers have lost their autonomy really by being heavily involved with the medical approach. It is bound to be harder to state an opinion in conflict to a psychiatrist and a team with which you have to work very closely. (Revans, 2003, p 30)

Impact on communication

In developing ways of working together, it is important that professionals find practical ways to communicate with each other and to work together across agencies. Multi-agency working can have both a positive and a negative impact on how well professionals communicate with each other.

In our interviews, good communication between agencies and professionals was recognised as key to the success of multi-agency working:

> "We can quite easily block inter-agency working can't we, quite easily, it has nothing to do with our profession at all; it is to do with how we engage and communicate with others really, directly or indirectly."

Professionals across the sites reported that as a result of multi-agency working, there were significant improvements in communicating with other professionals. Generally, professionals said that they were easier to get hold of, easier to access information from and that the structures of multi-agency teams/services improved formal opportunities for information sharing and problem solving.

> "It makes agencies talk to one another. You have to work across those boundaries which can be quite set."

> "It cuts down a huge amount of duplication when other professionals are there. Sometimes we can short-cut outpatients – go straight to the consultant

for an opinion. Cuts down on phone calls. Makes things more efficient and easier."

Some of the more formal structures that multi-agency services had put in place (such as regular meetings, steering groups, and so on) also formalised these positive opportunities for communication. On the whole, staff were committed to attending meetings, so knew that there would be a fixed time to focus on particular children:

> "It gives us registered 'time out' to meet and talk. It puts boundaries on it – here is 45 minutes to talk about one particular child."

As well as a reported overall improvement in communication between professionals and agencies, some difficulties remained.

There was concern about the possible duplication of multi-agency fora and the challenges that this posed to good communication. In each site other statutory assessments (looked after children, statementing of special education needs, record of needs) also led to multi-agency meetings. Some professionals were concerned that an additional multi-agency forum and meeting was creating another round of meetings for themselves and families.

There was also a recognition that information from assessments, care plans and reviews were not always being shared across agencies and that some professionals continued to do their own assessments, care plans and reviews in isolation from other agencies. A community nurse with specialist skills with children with complex health care needs acknowledged that she carried out a needs assessment for children without consulting any other professionals, but recognised the need to change this.

A number of teams/services had members who said that they would like their experience and views to be more effectively 'fed upwards' to commissioners and policy makers. Teams felt that they had acquired a broad range of knowledge about services and service delivery across agencies, based on strong relationships with families and children. They felt that this information and expertise could be used more productively in planning services and providing better and more responsive services. For example, a short breaks worker who also acted as a keyworker said:

> "We play a big part in families' lives. We want to be heard more. We can pass on our opinions and thoughts to a certain level but then we are ignored."

The desire to feed information up to more senior managers was also in order to highlight what was perceived to be the extra-ordinary needs of children with complex health care needs that might be underestimated by managers:

> "We need to prove that these families need more – at the moment they're seen as a pain and an expense. But our role has got to be flagging them up so they don't get forgotten."

In the same site a professional said that the service needed to develop more 'executive clout', so that instead of just making recommendations about levels of services they should be instrumental in setting them. This would require more financial power, including holding a joint budget.

Impact on workload

It is interesting to note that those staff who acted as keyworkers did not report a detrimental impact on their ability to manage their workload. In fact some staff felt that the role made things more efficient, because they often had a much better overview of the issues facing the family they coordinated for.

> "Being a coordinator gives you extra information about children that you wouldn't have as just a clinician. You get copied into all correspondence about a child, which means you know so much more about how things are working out for them. It has an inevitable impact on the quality of your own service."

Professionals with a keyworker role routinely said that it was part of what they would normally do and had always done in their existing role and for this reason perceived no adverse impacts on their workloads. However, senior managers had more concerns about workload and were surprised to learn in feedback from the research team that keyworkers were not unduly worried about this aspect of the impact of multi-agency working.

There did not seem to be clear guidelines for how much time a keyworker would devote to families with keyworkers being more likely to be responsive to parents' demands. This led several keyworkers to comment on the inequitable division of their time between families. As one social worker and keyworker put it:

> "Twenty per cent [of families] demand 80% of my time – the 'hard core families'. I have to put it in my diary to ring Mr and Mrs Quiet."

The amount of time keyworkers gave to families was often related to the particular needs of families. One keyworker talked about her time commitment with one family:

> "I sometimes think it would be easier to take her home and look after her myself! I am so involved at the moment – at her home every day."

Lack of adequate, 'ring-fenced' time and funding may mean that workers are asked to take part in new joint initiatives in addition to their main job. Consequently, difficulties can arise due to time constraints and a lack of priority being given to the additional role. Mukherjee et al (1999) indicate that where staff volunteer to take part in multi-agency work, they are more likely to feel positive about the new, or additional, role. However, insufficient time, in particular, can be an insurmountable barrier to effective joint work (Lacey, 1997). Our interviews suggested that staff working directly with families felt that their work was an extension of previous joined-up working, which had been formalised and therefore did not represent a significant increase in workload. However, a group of professionals in one site did not share this view and had opted out of being keyworkers. There was also a recognition that keyworkers could only take on the role for a limited number of families.

Impact on relationships with other professionals and agencies

A recurring theme in sites was how relationships had been improved on a professional and personal level. Professionals at several sites highlighted the improvement in relationships, saying that the 'blame culture' had gone. Staff had got to know each other better and as a result enjoyed working with each other more:

> "No one tries to steal anyone's thunder any more which does make a difference."

In one site the whole of a team that spanned several disciplines were accommodated in one building. Staff there found this very advantageous:

> "We're all here together. We know each other well. We can all help each other with problems. I can talk to an expert at a moment's notice."

The exposure to other peer professionals in meetings also meant that, as some staff highlighted, it encouraged them to make sure that they carried out tasks that they said they would, because it would be embarrassing not to.

> "There's a subtle peer pressure. It's helpful. You feel you can't turn up and say you haven't done stuff."

Joint recruitment was seen as a good way of improving links and relationships between agencies. This typically involved two agencies working together to draw up a job description and sit on the interview panel.

Nevertheless, some barriers routinely remained between agencies and professionals. Community health staff at one service said doctors and consultants in acute settings were unapproachable and did not take account of their views. In the same site, community social workers said there was insufficient dialogue with hospital social workers around the transition from hospital to home. Social workers in this site did not feel medical professionals took their views seriously. They also reported poor relationships and conflict with Education staff, who they did not feel were committed to join in multi-agency practice. In a site that employed large numbers of carers to provide home-based support to children with complex health care needs, carers highlighted a lack of effective communication between the service's staff and carers.

At service D, a particular group of professionals had refused to take on the role of being a keyworker because they had felt it to be outside of their remit.

This had been difficult for other professionals to accept. One existing keyworker said:

> "My personal view is that it only works if we all pitch in a bit ... if we share the load."

Education was, in every service except one, mentioned as the agency with whom it was *least* easy to work with in multi-agency practice. This was not a universal statement about Education staff as a whole; many individuals within Education were thought to be committed and helpful. In one service, for example, special schools staff were said to be keen to work collaboratively, and the multi-agency process was line managed by an Education manager. However, the very clear statutory framework that Education has and the fact that staff that know children best (teachers and classroom assistants) were generally unavailable to take part in meetings meant that Education was perceived as the least accessible partner.

At service E, the absence of staff from Education at multi-agency meetings who really knew the children well was thought to be particularly difficult for children who were at the point of transition. Educational psychologists were most likely to attend meetings, but other professionals said they would have preferred other Education staff who knew children better to attend instead. Interestingly, in this site, the educational psychologist felt that multi-agency meetings were not beneficial to Education staff who knew children intimately, because other professionals had less to tell them.

Professionals in three sites reported difficulties in getting Health as an agency to take an active interest and commit to the multi-agency project. In service A, one senior manager felt that the emphasis on keyworking had focused on staff and services in the community and that hospitals were only beginning to think about how to work in a more coordinated way. In this site there were significant barriers reported in working with Health. This was, in part, due to the restructuring of health authorities. There was criticism of a perceived intransigence of Health to expand on their role to take on board a more coordinated approach:

"They [Health] have been trained to work that way at the end of the day, they haven't been trained to work in a multi-agency way."

In this service, concern was expressed about whether or not colleagues in Health were motivated and interested in taking on the principles of the project. The example was given of the project manager addressing a group of Health professionals:

"I am a little embarrassed sometimes by the response.... If she were talking about a specific medical thing they would be very interested, they could see it as their domain, see it directly related to them and they would want to be heavily involved in it. As it involves the area of work it does, she gets her 20 minutes, she says her bit and then it's the next item on the agenda, that's very interesting ... she was given an attentive 20 minutes but at the end of that they had no real idea about how we as a department would identify children to go onto the service coordination list ... it developed no great interest ... there is no real enthusiasm to really go for it."

There was an acknowledgement that it was difficult to win Health funding for an initiative like keyworking, because it is never at the top of the agenda:

"I see no willingness in this trust to orientate money that has previously been spent in hospital in-patient care to a more community care package. I see no evidence of that at all."

Service F was based in a hospital setting and here a senior manager in Health said that the development of the multi-agency service had helped her to think more about the needs of disabled children 'beyond the hospital walls'. There had been a change in attitude in other hospital nursing staff too. This manager described instances where nursing staff would now think twice about discharging children when consultants have said, 'this child can go home', without appropriate equipment being available at home.

Barriers remained between certain professionals and certain agencies. When we look at some of the literature on partnership working, this is probably unsurprising. Banks (2002) argues that it is not possible to assume that putting structures of multi-agency work in place will automatically lead to effective partnership and collaboration between professionals. Banks also reports that in partnerships for particular groups there may routinely be a *reticent partner*, that is an agency/partner who is less willing to play an active role and passes responsibility onto the others.

Commitment to multi-agency working meant that professionals continued to work hard at sustaining and improving communication between agencies and professionals. And there was an acknowledgment that working in new ways that challenge traditional boundaries can be difficult. One professional described the inherent difficulties:

"Only when people don't understand what we do and how. Then we just push it with people gently. If they say 'no we can't do that, we've never done it before, it's not our job' – we say 'well neither have we. Let's do it together and meet each other halfway'. We're always coming up against challenges – things that we've never done before."

Impact on service provision within and across agencies

In service A, one senior manager talked about the impact of the service on other multi-agency initiatives. In this site, a 'school entry plan' had been devised for children with complex health care needs starting school. The plan, which brought together all the main agencies, looked at individual education plans, but also whether any physical adaptations were required at the school. It also addressed staff training. The manager attributed the development of this to the success of the existing multi-agency work:

"These are the sorts of spin-offs that you see from a project like this."

In each of the sites, senior managers hoped that the principles of communication and coordination that had been developed would be extended to the work of other agencies, in other projects, relating to disabled children and services for children and young people in general.

Structural changes in agencies were often seen as an opportunity to build on the multi-agency practice that had been established, for example in the development of Children's Trusts. However, some managers were concerned that not everyone knew about the multi-agency work and that professionals in other services might start from scratch, rather than building on what was happening in the existing multi-agency service.

The multi-agency services, which are the focus of this research, demonstrated some effective partnerships between professionals and varying degrees of commitment from different agencies. However, most of the services had futures that were not always certain. Other developments in service planning and provision did not always take account of what had been learnt by the multi-agency team/service.

Impact on work and relationships with families

We have seen that professionals spoke highly of their experiences of working in a multi-agency service; they enjoyed it and found it rewarding. The overwhelming majority of professionals said that they were committed to and enthusiastic about the principles and practice of multi-agency working. The most commonly used words to describe the experience of working in a multi-agency service were, 'rewarding', 'enjoyable', 'challenging', 'motivating' and 'satisfying'. This quote from a keyworker is a typical one:

> "It improves the quality of our work lives. We give ourselves do'able tasks and do them."

However, in a cautionary note, Banks writes that there is not enough focus on ensuring that joint working results in positive outcomes for the people that the work is supposed to benefit:

> All the effort goes into setting up the teams and sometimes you can lose sight of whether they are delivering a truly integrated service along the lines of what the client wants." (Banks, quoted in Snell, 2003, p 28)

From the professionals' point of view, they thought that the structures of their multi-agency services created better and more effective ways to coordinate

support and services for families and to coordinate contact with professionals. For example, the team meetings in service E were routinely described by professionals as an effective forum for families to have their problems resolved promptly and efficiently. A speech and language therapist and coordinator in this site described how a family was having problems with adaptations to their home. The family wrote to the Chair of the monthly multi-agency meeting, explaining the problem. As a result the Chair wrote to all the professionals represented at the meeting saying how important it was for the adaptations to be sorted out quickly, and as a result they were.

Professionals across sites talked about 'reductions in duplication' and professionals in five of the six services felt that considerable improvements had been made in coordinating planning for discharge from hospital.

Professionals felt that their relationships were enhanced with families because they were offering more coordinated services. They said that they respected and took account of parents' views about day-to-day care issues. They remarked frequently on the pressures that families faced and expressed admiration for their resilience.

Professionals said that working closely with families gave them clearer insights into the issues associated with having a child with complex health care needs. An occupational therapist talked about what she had learnt from attending a training event in which parents had shared some of their experiences:

> "The part of the training I found most useful was when parents said how they felt when people keep asking them questions. I felt appalled at what we do to parents. We don't mean to. But we just don't think about it. It helped to focus my thoughts on how we can do better for families. I spend a lot of time being a manager of a service – I need to step back and remember the child and the family."

Professionals at one service talked about the work as fundamentally changing the relationships between themselves and parents by giving parents more power. A senior manager acknowledged that this change was not easy:

"It is very scary I am sure, for some professionals to feel that their power shift is to change. So they do need to be coached and supported in making that shift, and for some it will be really difficult to do, but by actually bringing the opportunity to openly share that fear and then be able to move on from it..."

Professionals liked the fact that they appeared as a more coherent and professional team and felt that this would enable families to perceive that they were all working together towards the same goals. For some staff, however, this enabled them to present a united front *against* certain parents:

"For difficult families it is useful for them to see that we all talk to each other – that they can't play us off against each other."

"... and where some families in the past might have played professionals off against each other this is more difficult now as [multi-agency teams] enable us to be open and honest and to say, 'I'm having a particular problem with this mum'. We feel more confident about discussing difficult issues."

Several professionals said that a multi-agency approach to working with families meant that the way services were delivered was more transparent to families. It was possible for families to see and understand that there were limits to what was on offer. A social worker who acted as a key worker for a family said:

"They're realistic about what we can and can't do. They know there are no magic wands."

And a physiotherapist stated that:

"[The multi-agency meeting] give families a realistic forum for raising issues. We are all saying the same thing to them in a consistent way. They are hearing the same message. Some families said they didn't know what was available and now they are less demanding as they know the reality of what resources we have within our power to offer them."

The issue of advocacy was a recurring theme in interviews with professionals. Most professionals described this as a difficult role to get right for families and some said they would not take it:

"The advocacy part of the role is actually quite minimal. But it can be the most difficult. When you are a clinician already and you have to say things on behalf of a family to other clinicians that may imply criticism – this can be hard. Families are often 'accusing' people of not being there or not putting in as much input as they'd like. Sometimes this is true, sometimes it can be more a perception on the families' part. So you can end up being more of a negotiator – a middle-man – between families and colleagues."

A major concern about taking on an advocacy role was that it could cause damage to relationships between professionals or agencies. One professional said about being asked by families to advocate for them:

"I've been invited to do that by families and I haven't done it. I've steered them towards SCOPE or the parent-partnership scheme. Am I too chicken? I think it's a separate function and they are better placed to do it than me. I think they're more effective at it. I represent Health so if they have a problem with Education, for example, then it becomes Health versus Education."

Professionals, most often in the context of families wanting additional resources or services, discussed the role of advocate. Relationships between professionals and parents were most strained when a professional was asked by families to ask their own and other agencies for more. A social work team leader discussed the difficult position her staff faced when they came to her to ask for additional resources, only to find a negative answer:

"... and then the social worker goes back to the family and the family says, 'you're not advocating for me strongly enough'. But I can't overspend on the budget."

A group of social workers in one of the services described poor relationships with families and talked about withholding information from parents about their entitlements because they knew that the money and services would not be there to meet their needs/ entitlements. They talked about this as 'protecting parents' and said that it was difficult to support families because resources were so scarce and that the 'joy of the job had gone'.

Professionals interpreted families' critical responses to services in different ways. A minority said that some families were defensive and difficult to work with and that there was unwillingness on some parents' part to accept their child's disability. Again, a small number talked about parents fighting for resources as an expression of stress and anxiety. A keyworker said:

"Parents saying they want more respite or more physio, for example, is the stress that they are under becoming manifest in wanting tangible things – it becomes their focus. They express their distress by coming out fighting. It's something they can count. We as link workers risk fuelling that if we don't understand what's going on there."

One multi-agency service provided families with packages of home-based care so that their children could be discharged from hospitals. It was suggested that families would probably always ask for more support, because they could never anticipate what life would be like once their child was discharged. The hospital ward manager commented:

"Parents are so keen to get their families home that they say they can cope with a basic package, but then they get home and it's a different reality so they begin to ask for more. As they get more they think, 'oh I like this', and they want more. They have to come to terms with the complexities of their life."

Professionals' perspectives on their relationships with disabled children and young people

Professionals who worked directly with families gave positive and warm narrative accounts about the children and young people who they worked with and for. However, there was not very much evidence of strong, individual relationships between professionals and disabled children and young people with complex health care needs.

Professionals said that a lack of time and barriers associated with communication impairments were the two main reasons for this:

"It's a bit of a luxury now to think about having meaningful individual relationships with children."

Additionally, many professionals said that they thought another professional had an existing strong relationship with the child, but often we did not find this to be the case. Another reason given by some professionals for the focus of their relationship being on the parent as opposed to the child was that parents wanted this to be the case. A social worker and keyworker said that they tried to establish a separate relationship with children and young people as they got older, but that parents could sometimes impede this:

"Parents miss the point that we work with and for their children too. They think we're just there for them. It's hard because ultimately you are only there with parental agreement so you can't push it too hard."

Most professionals admitted that this was an area of weakness, although one keyworker felt that some of the children had such complex needs that she could not see a role for building relationships with them at all. One site had appointed a member of staff specifically to work with young people around increasing their participation. This professional was responsible for fostering individual relationships as well as feeding messages from children and young people to other colleagues and managers:

"Key workers see the whole picture whereas I focus on the child or young person."

There were a small number of staff, however, who demonstrated that they did have a positive relationship with individual children. One community nurse described how she interacted with one child who does not use words. In her role as keyworker for the child and the family, she used objects of reference so that the child might know that it was her – most often she used her ring. She also played her recorder and sang with the child to try to get a sense of whether or not she was happy.

Professionals' views on the overall impact on families

The overwhelming majority of professionals in each site thought that the service was making a positive difference to families' quality of life. While the difference was thought to be positive in that things were assumed to be better than they had been in the past, the change was not assumed to be significant for families' quality of life:

> "It's not a significant difference to quality of life. More coordination of what is already happening. Families are not getting things they weren't getting before. It's just better coordinated now. It pulls things together and makes them more effective."

A keyworker reflected on whether the service was making things better for families:

> "I don't know. It's really tricky. I don't know if some families feel it really makes a difference. Maybe it's just seen as another meeting. But I do think that problems are highlighted more quickly and sorted out by less people."

> "I hope it's making things better for families. I don't know how many parents would say this is the case though."

> "I think it is making things better for families and children though I'm not sure all families are happy – some will always want more."

> "... one hopes they would say things like it's made life not quite so frenetic."

The most discernable difference was that children with complex health care needs were having their health needs met in a home/community setting:

> "I think you can see a marked difference in the deployment of services say from two or three years ago."

At service F, professionals and managers felt that the biggest difference that the service had made was that it prevented children having to stay in hospital. Children could be at home and accessing school. However, the impact of this on families as a whole was routinely referred to.

Although, as discussed, professionals reported positive outcomes for themselves and their agencies, there was still concern about whether it had worked as well for families. In one service, it was felt that this absence of any additional funding for new or existing services meant that families' expectations had been unfairly

raised. It was not possible to deliver on the care plan written with and for families. There was also concern expressed by a small number of professionals about the absence of new or additional services. A senior manager reflected on families' disappointment about this:

> "... plan upon plan upon plan but no actual difference in services and you can sense the frustration."

In service A, it was suggested that although there was good multi-agency working at senior management level, things were not necessarily as joined up for direct care/support staff:

> "I do see there is a significant, a real policy about working together, multi-agency working at senior management level. How it evolves down to middle management and most importantly to grass roots, I refer to grass roots as those social workers and health visitors who actually have first-hand contact with families, I am not so sure that the families see that it is working because I still hear families say, 'don't these agencies ever talk to each other?' and that comes up consistently in consultation even now, 'why can't the agencies talk to each other?'."

Very few professionals reflected on whether their service was making things better specifically for children and young people. Just one professional who had a specialist role to enhance social and leisure opportunities for children and young people was able to comment on the impact of multi-agency working on children and young people themselves:

> "Making things better? – yes I see the difference in the increase in confidence of young people. They go from recluse to completely out-going and enjoy going out with me. Parents say it's the best thing they've done."

Summary

- Working in multi-agency services provided professionals with *enhanced opportunities for personal and professional development*. Staff said they learnt more about each other's roles and as a result felt more efficient in meeting families' needs. There was also greater insight into the work cultures of other agencies and formal and informal structures, which enabled agencies to look jointly at common problems and issues.

- Being part of a multi-agency team had the potential to *broaden professionals' sense of role and identity*. Some services had created new labels to describe roles for staff in a multi-agency context, but there was not always clarity about the nature of these. Some staff welcomed the expansion of their role to help support families with a broad range of responses. Professionals talked about becoming more *generic*. But there were some professionals, especially senior managers, who had some concerns about the erosion of expertise and specialisms. Social workers were unclear of their role in what they perceived to be a medically dominated arena.

- In terms of *communication*, there were broadly positive outcomes for multi-agency services. Staff said there were clearer and more efficient channels of communication. However, some problems remained, including aspects of service provision that were not 'joined up' and poorer communication between direct care staff and senior managers.

- Multi-agency work *did not appear to have a detrimental impact on the workload* of professionals, despite the concerns of managers that it would. There did not seem to be clear guidelines for all staff on how much time commitment should be made available to the services.

- *Relationships between different staff groups and different agencies* were reported to have improved markedly. Formal structures, which brought people together, were thought to be especially helpful. Some problems remained, due to different statutory frameworks, incompatible IT systems and a lack of commitment from some agencies and individuals.

- There were some examples of the *transfer of good practice* around multi-agency working to other services and across agencies. However, examples of duplication and disconnection between different services also remained problematic.

- *Working with families* as part of a multi-agency team was said by professionals to be enjoyable and rewarding. They said that they enjoyed stronger and better informed relationships with parents and could be more effective in supporting them. Some staff said they were able to be more united *against* parents who were perceived to be difficult. Relationships between staff and families were problematic in the areas of advocacy and scarce/limited resources. There were very few examples of strong individual relationships between professionals and disabled children and young people. Lack of time and barriers relating to communication were cited as the reasons for this.

- Overall, professionals were almost unanimous in their belief that the *multi-agency services they worked in were making a positive difference to the lives of families*. The fact that children with complex health care needs were, in the main, at home and not in hospital was thought to be an important indicator of success. However, many professionals felt that families might not describe a significant difference in their lives as a result of the service, given the relative lack of any new or additional resources or services.

4

Exploring the impact of multi-agency working on families' daily lives and well-being

Multi-agency working, as exemplified by the six sites described in this report, has the potential to make significant differences to the way that families and children experience services, and to their overall quality of life. This chapter draws on the findings from our interviews with 25 families caring for a child with complex health care needs. We examine this material in terms of the evidence it provides about the impact of the multi-agency services on daily family life and well-being. The impact of multi-agency working on families' contact with professionals will be discussed in Chapter 5, and Chapter 6 will focus on the experiences of children with complex health care needs themselves.

Defining the impact of multi-agency services on family quality of life

It is well established in the research literature that disabled children and their families experience a multitude of disabling barriers that prevent them from accessing adequate support and services, and from participating fully in society (Watson et al, 2002). In order to overcome these barriers, research shows (Turnbull et al, 2000) that children and families need focused and coordinated support in the following areas relating to their quality of life:

- *daily family life* – mealtimes, sleep, travel, household chores, providing care, managing disabled children's health care needs at home;
- *physical environment* – accessibility of housing, outdoor space and local community buildings;
- *financial well-being* – sources of income (job, benefits), money management;

- *social well-being* – leisure, holidays, relationships, social support;
- *emotional well-being* – awareness of sources of family pressure, stress management, sense of control;
- *skills and learning* – access by child and family to school, college and other sources of personal development;
- *contact with services and professionals* – access to services, communicating with professionals, coordination of services and professionals.

Our interviews with families focused on the support that they received from the multi-agency services in helping them to overcome barriers in each of the seven areas listed above. Given that each of the six multi-agency services had aims that sought to tackle some of these barriers, as well as to coordinate and to facilitate better access to services, we were particularly interested to find out more about families' experiences. We were also interested to compare our data about these current experiences, collected in a context where multi-agency services were set up with the aim of achieving positive change for families, with the largely negative experiences of families of disabled children (including children with complex health care needs) chronicled in previous research studies (Sloper and Turner, 1992; Kirk and Glendinning, 1999; Townsley and Robinson, 2000), collected mainly in a context where specific multi-agency working for this group was absent. With all this in mind, we asked, therefore, what positive differences, if any, were the six multi-agency services making to families' daily lives and sense of well-being.

Daily family life

Previous research has highlighted that families of disabled children are likely to be experiencing difficulties with daily routines such as sleeping, mealtimes, and travel (Roberts and Lawton, 2001). For families caring for a disabled child who also has complex health care needs, other difficulties associated with managing their child's health care at home may also be an issue (Townsley and Robinson, 2000).

Night disturbance and sleep loss

Seventeen of the 25 families we interviewed revealed that they experienced considerable night disturbance, with several families reporting that their child woke them at least six times a night. Despite this, only six families had received specific help at night-time from the multi-agency service, either in terms of a carer who stayed overnight in the family home, or via short breaks away from home for the child to enable family members to have a good night's sleep.

Three additional families were receiving support at night from other sources – from relatives and friends, or from a voluntary agency. Two families told us that they had received support in the past, but this had been withdrawn, in one case because it was a pilot scheme that had not been continued because of funding difficulties. Seven families reported that they had never received, or been offered, support for night disturbance, and of these, three families specifically stated that they would like help.

The effects of regular sleep deprivation on family health and well-being was highlighted by several respondents and is likely to have a detrimental impact on overall family quality of life:

> "We get up to her every night, six times last night ... every so often you think I just can't cope any more, but you do because you've got to, but yes, people just think they go to bed and that's the end of it."

> "What was happening was I was up and down and up and down. You couldn't always hear her breathing over her baby monitor you see and that is why they thought my heart was, an irregular heart beat, because the sleep deprivation was causing it."

These experiences are shared by many families caring for a disabled child and have been have been well documented and highlighted in the research literature in this field. Kirk and Glendinning (1999) note that sleep loss is a regular occurrence for carers of technology-dependent children and is attributed to various factors including anxiety about the child's condition, false monitor alarms, or the need to remain vigilant over the child in the night. Townsley and Robinson (2000) found that three quarters of the families involved in their research reported regular episodes of night disturbance as a direct result of their children's need for tube feeding.

Family routines and household chores

For families of children with complex health care needs, family routines, such as mealtimes, household chores, toileting, getting up and going to bed, can involve lengthier and more complex sets of tasks. Without additional support at these particular times, parents may struggle to meet the demands of all family members and may find that they have time for little else, including being available to interact with their disabled child (Redmond, 2000).

Of the 25 families we spoke to, only two were receiving support (from carers coming to the family home) at mealtimes. However, four families reported that they had received advice and training about managing mealtimes, which they had found helpful in finding ways to alleviate some of the extra pressures at these times. There was very little evidence of support being offered at other times, or for household chores. One family reported receiving six hours' 'home help' per week and another family in the same area had been offered some short-term help with ironing. Another family had actually turned down the offer of support to cook meals as they felt this degree of input would be too intrusive.

Overall, however, support with family routines and household chores was not an area in which families appeared to need significant input. Indeed two families said that this was the one area of their lives where they felt they had some control, and could feel *organised*.

Travel and transport

For children with complex health care needs and their families, transport can be a difficult and complicated issue to contend with. Our findings showed transport and travel was not an area where advice or support was readily forthcoming from multi-agency services. We were told about just four examples of multi-agency services providing specific advice about transport, or offering support in terms of access to taxis or helping with Motability claims.

"My son has a taxi to and from school, and they have a taxi suitable for wheelchair access, and for some reason they suddenly decided they were going to use that one on a different run and they would send a car, so I had to fold up the wheelchair, and all the hassle that goes with it and I mentioned it to [service coordinator] and she said 'oh that's alright' and off she went and phoned the advisory teacher who then phoned County Hall and then, by the evening, the wheelchair taxi appeared again, and that was brilliant because something like that can cause a lot of pressure and it was all sorted, and that, I was very impressed with."

Overall, however, there was little evidence of a proactive or consistent approach to this area of support to families. Interviews revealed a very patchy picture of provision, with some parents finding out about schemes such as Motability by chance, sometimes several years after they became eligible.

Other stories emerged, such as the two families who had been acting as daily escorts for their respective children on school transport, as no one suitable had been found to take on this role. Also the family who had to use their own car to transport their child's wheelchair to, and from, school as the school bus did not have enough room to take it on board. In all three of these examples, without such a high and committed level of personal input from their families, the children concerned would not have been able to access statutory education.

Managing complex health care in the family home

Many parents of children with complex health care needs must quickly learn a whole new set of caring skills, many of which will be technically and medically complex. Previous research (Kirk and Glendinning, 1999; Noyes, 1999b; Townsley and Robinson, 2000) has highlighted that lack of training and support in the community once a child has been discharged from hospital with a complex medical intervention is a common occurrence. Previous research has also found that inadequate supplies and inappropriate or faulty medical equipment have been at the root of many problems and may have been the result of poor communication between professionals, or lack of agreement over funding, particularly where equipment is unusual and expensive.

In contrast to previous research findings, we found that families were receiving support that enabled them to adequately manage their children's complex health care needs at home. Two of the sites had been established with a specific remit to meet this area of child and family need. But even in the other, more generic sites, services appeared to be providing focused support for families in terms of managing children's complex health care needs at home, and particularly in terms of helping to organise equipment and supplies.

"They have liaised with the paediatric nursing team, whether it be to do with the training for carers ... or sometimes ... [keyworker] has said 'well I am going to contact them' and I say 'well when you do, can you put in my order for syringes, mouth swabs and things like that?'."

"There was a particular time when [keyworker] sorted out getting the right amount of feeds, because I was ordering so much liquid feed ... and somebody had reduced it saying I was stock-piling the stuff. I saw my GP and she said 'well, we don't like people storing up two months of stuff' and I said 'well personally I would rather go out and buy it all at Sainsbury's but this is the situation'. So anyway [keyworker] did sort that out and we were allowed a month's feed on prescription again."

A few families, however, did highlight that problems such as waiting lists and arguments over funding were still issues when it came to equipment.

"We need things quickly and there's often a wait and I have to ring around to get things."

Several families described a feeling of being 'thrown in at the deep end' when their child was discharged from hospital. This was particularly the case for two families who felt that they had not been given sufficient information about the likely impact of their child's medical intervention on family quality of life.

"At the beginning no one explained that so many people would be visiting and phoning and that there would be so many appointments in the house. No one told me what to expect, I'd like to have known more."

Indeed, for one of these families, information provision had been so inadequate that the family had felt sufficiently confident about the likely impact on their home life to turn down a 24-hour package of care, a decision, that in retrospect, they had greatly regretted.

"In hindsight perhaps we should have said yes at the beginning, but it was so new to us, and we had no idea what we were letting ourselves in for. It would have been good to revisit the thought a few months in, but no one asked us again."

Although there was no doubt that taking on the responsibility of managing overtly medical procedures was a huge additional burden for most parents of children with complex health care needs, overall, families did not report such a high degree of dissatisfaction with support for this area of daily family life as has been noted in previous research (for example Kirk and Glendinning, 1999; Townsley and Robinson, 2000). Of all areas relating to quality of life, support with managing complex health needs, particularly in terms of providing training (for parents and carers) and equipment to enable a child to live at home, and to attend school on a regular basis, was probably the one in which there were fewest concerns or expressions of need; a remarkable achievement considering the complexity of the health needs of this group of children.

Physical environment

Living in unsuitable housing makes it harder for families to care for their disabled child (Oldman and Beresford, 1998; Beresford and Oldman, 2000) and is a significant barrier to enjoying essential childhood

experiences such as moving around the house, playing, taking part in family life and learning to look after oneself. For children with complex health care needs, the presence of technological/medical equipment in the family home is likely to require more space than the average family home can provide (Townsley and Robinson, 2000). Many children with complex health care needs need space not only for their own particular equipment (for example feeding pump, or oxygen canisters), but may also require specially adapted furniture and a hoist system to enable them to be comfortable and to move around the house.

Almost all of the families we spoke to had either made, or were planning, adaptations to their home, in order to accommodate wheelchairs or other equipment needed by their disabled child. Planning, organising and funding adaptations is a complex business, often involving liaison with numerous professionals from different agencies. As such, it is a key area where input from a named person, such as a keyworker, could reduce the burden on families and help to resolve housing problems. However, the interviews we conducted with families showed that when they did get support in this area, it was largely mediated by an occupational therapist, who sometimes played a coordinating role and sometimes did not. This is not a surprising finding, and yet given the emphasis on a named person acting as a keyworker in four of the sites, we might have expected to see more evidence of their input in this area.

Overall, four families out of 25 reported receiving specific input from a keyworker in terms of housing and adaptations. Several people said that they did not think advice and support on this issue was part of their keyworkers role. And another family described a situation where their keyworker was happy to give advice, but was not able to progress the application for adaptations, due to her lack of seniority in terms of getting access to resources. There was one example of a family having to wait four years to get the adaptations they needed and they felt forgotten by the multi-agency service in this respect.

The interviews with families also highlighted how much work they did themselves around adaptations. Families were found to have built ramps themselves and paid for their own stair lifts. One family took out a personal loan to make adaptations to their home. One family even purpose-built their own home to suit their child's needs, and two families had moved to purpose-built homes provided by housing associations.

Families we spoke to highlighted that where advice and funding for adaptations was not forthcoming, they were forced to resort to self-financing to improve the situation. In itself, this is an alarming finding, but is even more shocking if we consider that nearly three quarters of these families had incomes below the national average.

Financial well-being

Previous research has shown that families of disabled children often face unacceptable levels of poverty and are unable to spend enough to meet the needs of their families (JRF, 1999; Dobson et al, 2001). Many families do not receive their full benefit entitlements, particularly Black and minority ethnic families (Chamba et al, 1999). Dobson and Middleton (1998) describe the many *little things* that contribute to significantly increased costs for families of disabled children. For families with a child with complex health care needs, costs are likely to be even higher and may include additional items such as transport to regional hospitals for appointments or in an emergency, extra equipment and toys, higher cost of utilities such as heating and lighting when the child is at home for long periods, and so on. In addition, parents and carers of disabled children with complex health care needs experience immense barriers to employment. These barriers include employers failing to take parents' caring responsibility into account, lack of flexible support to allow parents to take on work, and the assumption by many schools and hospitals that parents do not work (JRF, 1999).

Family income

The total household incomes of the 25 families were given in Table 4, Chapter 1 and are repeated here.

Comparing these figures with the national picture, where the average national gross total household income is approximately £25,000 (based on figures for 1999-2000, ONS, 2000), it is clear that the

Table 4: Income status of families interviewed

Gross family income (including benefits)	Number of families
£5,000-£9,999	5
£10,000-£14,999	7
£15,000-£19,999	2
£20,000-£24,999	4
£25,000-£34,999	2
£35,000-£49,999	3
£50,000-£74,999	0
£75,000-£99,999	1
Missing data	1

majority (18) of the families in the study had an income that was below the national average. This being the case, it is perhaps surprising that 18 families reported that they had never been offered help with general money matters (advice on benefits is discussed separately below). Just one family talked about a financial assessment carried out by their keyworker. One other family thought that they could talk to their keyworker if they wanted to. Only two families expressed no concerns or worries about money.

Support and advice on claiming benefits entitlements

We asked families who had offered them advice on claiming benefits entitlements. Eight families had received help from a social worker and a further three had sought advice from their local Citizens' Advice Bureau. Only three families said they had either received help with advice about benefits from their keyworker or that they would go to this person for help. Overall, then, just under half of the families we interviewed reported receiving benefits advice via the multi-agency service. Indeed, three families said that they did all the work themselves regarding benefits, with one family stating that this had been:

"A complete, stressful nightmare."

Given the relatively low incomes of the majority of the families that were interviewed, this finding is alarming. Moreover, given the potentially pivotal role that a keyworker plays in a family's life, providing information about benefits and supporting families to make claims would appear to be an important aspect of this role, and one which could make a substantial positive difference to the financial well-being of this group.

Employment

The difficulties that parents of disabled children face regarding employment are frequently documented in the research literature (for example Kagan et al, 1998). Only six of the primary family carers we interviewed had paid work, and this was in four cases very part-time in order to fit around the needs of their child (see Table 7). A further two carers were foster parents and considered caring for their child to be their employment. Six parents stated that they could not work because of their child's needs and the effect that working would have on their benefits. A further three families said that they would like to work, but there was no suitable, available childcare. Two mothers did some part-time voluntary work.

However, comparing these figures with data on 5,376 families with severely disabled children drawn from the Family Fund database, it is clear that the mothers that we visited had a higher rate of employment than the wider group of families of disabled children. In our study we found that 32% of mothers had some sort of paid work (including foster caring). The fathers had a 58% rate of employment, which is similar to the general picture. The Family Fund data is taken from all families with disabled children who had applied to the Fund and who were living within the geographical areas covered by the six multi-agency services. These figures showed an employment rate of 60% of fathers, 12% of part-time mothers and 3% of full-time mothers. It is not known whether this data includes foster caring, which might alter the picture.

It is difficult to know what sort of direct role multi-agency services could play in assisting parents and carers to find paid employment, although one parent told us that her keyworker had helped her to get driving lessons so that it would be easier for her to find work. *Indirectly*, however, the coordination of flexible and appropriate support (such as escorts, sitting services, or access to after-school clubs) is an obvious area for more focused input.

Many mothers, in particular, felt that they were very much *on call* 24 hours a day. Consequently, they felt unable to seek paid work as the need to be there to attend to their child's needs (for example if the child was taken ill at school) was paramount. In some cases, these families were also *plugging the gap* in terms of inadequate service provision, at the expense of their own personal financial well-being. For example, as we have mentioned, one parent told us that she had to act as a school escort for her daughter, since there was no one available with the necessary training to take on this task. This was a time-consuming and additional role for this parent, and further distanced her from seeking employment.

> "Because I'm an escort you see. I've been escorting her since she went to school, so that takes another hour and a half off my day, but I did it because obviously I wanted her to be taken to school safely."

Social well-being

It is well established in the literature that social exclusion is a huge barrier for disabled children and their families and is a direct result of a lack of flexible support from services. The presence of additional technical/medical equipment can make going out very difficult, or even impossible, for families of children with complex health care needs (Michaelis et al, 1992; Petr et al, 1995; Kirk and Glendinning, 1999; Townsley and Robinson, 2000; Mencap, 2003). Research shows that parents and carers want support that is flexible enough to respond to their particular families' needs, while children and young people want the same things as any young person – friends, money, a place to call their own and the freedom to do the things they enjoy doing (JRF, 1999; Morris, 1999; Murray, 2001).

Table 7: Employment status of families interviewed

Female carer working (paid)		Male carer working (paid)	
Yes, full-time	2	Yes	11
No	17	No	7 (2 for health reasons)
Part-time	4	Part time	0
Foster parent	2	Foster parent	1

Opportunities for social activities outside the family home

The families we interviewed all experienced major difficulties in finding and organising opportunities for themselves or their disabled child to enjoy a break or leisure activities. The interviews showed just how isolated many families felt, with nine families stating that that they were simply unable to go out without their disabled child.

> "I wish we had a normal life and we could do normal things all the time."

Holidays were thought by several (five) families to be too difficult to contemplate, so they just did not go. They talked of the problems with equipment and travelling with a child with complex health care needs and felt that it was not worth the effort. As one family said:

> "I don't think anyone could do anything more to help us have a holiday. It's too complex. [The multi-agency service] couldn't really sort it out. We are the only ones who really know how to look after her and when it's an emergency or not."

Seven families did have holidays (in some cases 'days out' rather than staying away from home) and some had received financial help for this, mostly from the Family Fund. One family told us how their keyworker had helped them to write letters for customs regarding the child's drugs in order for them to be able to travel abroad, but this was the only example of keyworkers being involved in this aspect of family life.

Almost without exception, the families we spoke to stressed the importance of taking holidays as a whole family, and consequently voiced feelings of guilt, or concern that this was not always possible, or understood by service providers:

> "It feels terrible to go on holiday and leave one of your kids behind, but after a few beers we had a good time and it was good for the other kids."

> "The professionals can't understand that we don't want her taken away from us, we just want a break away from the 'phone ringing all the time."

Sitting services and the provision of short breaks

The minimal, and in some cases, non-existent, provision of flexible and adequate sitting services or short breaks was thought by families to be largely responsible for the social isolation they faced.

In terms of sitting services, three of the families we interviewed had been linked with one or more carers for their child for sitting purposes. In general, however, the support offered to families in the form of carers tended to focus mainly on one-to-one help during the day for the child at school or nursery, or help during the night. Although valued, it was therefore of little benefit to families regarding their social lives. Where a sitting service was offered, except in one case, it was not what the family really wanted. The obvious need for the multi-agency services to organise staff rotas, and in several cases the difficulties experienced in recruiting carers, meant that the nature of this service tended to be very inflexible, and occasionally in itself was a cause of additional pressure.

One family, for example, felt they had to go out when the carer was there, whether they wanted to or not. For another family, although the timing of a sitting service (where a paid carer looked after the disabled child at home so the parents could go out) was not ideal, the family felt that the service was better than nothing, and that they should carry on using it, otherwise it would be taken away and they would be left with no time out whatsoever. In only one family had help explicitly been arranged by the keyworker so that the mother could go out in the evenings. Four families said that they would like a sitting service and a further two stated that there was nothing suitable for them. In the absence of sitting support from the multi-agency services, a large proportion of families (32% of those we interviewed) said they relied on relatives or friends to help out, but admitted that this too could be problematic and worrying.

Many families with disabled children rely heavily on short-break (respite) services. This type of service will either be provided by a residential centre or within another family's own home, with the carer being paid to look after the child for short, regular periods of time. However, six of the families that we interviewed stated that there was no suitable short-break provision for them in their area. A further two families had been offered short breaks via their keyworker, but they had not wanted what was being offered. A further four families had applied for short breaks, but were still waiting. For families caring for a child with complex health care needs, the difficulties often lay in the nature of the provision being offered, and the families' fears or misgivings about this:

> "I did manage to find a residential unit for [my daughter] to go to for three days, and I had a holiday with a friend who lives near the unit, but it was something I had arranged and found out about. The one place that was suggested that [child] could go to, when I had a look, I just thought, no, I wouldn't put her medically at risk, it just wasn't geared up for the sort of problem I know I had been experiencing with her, so I said no, it's not safe for her to be there, you check her once an hour, I don't think so, sometimes I can be up to her 20 times an hour."

The issue of finding home-based carers and sitters who are adequately trained and whose homes are appropriately adapted has been identified by previous research on support to children with complex health care needs (for example, Townsley and Robinson, 2000) and was still a big issue for the majority of the families we interviewed.

> "They have not got many carers that have got the houses that would be able to accommodate a child like ours."

Consequently, only four families reported accessing family-based short-breaks provision. Seven families were relying on residential provision, either in Health- or Social Services-run residential units (three families), or in children's hospices (four families). One family was using a combination of family-based and residential provision. Several families were critical of the care provided by residential units for their children:

> "The children just sleep and get drugs whereas at home we do all we can to amuse her."

Previous research (Robinson and Jackson, 1998) has questioned the suitability of children's hospices as primary providers of short breaks for disabled

children (who will not necessarily be life-threatened, or life-limited). In contrast, however, the families we spoke to all expressed their satisfaction with the services offered by hospices, and highlighted their child's enjoyment of the break offered:

> "We get 21 days respite from [children's hospice]. They are absolutely fantastic. We call it her sleepover place. It's time for her, away from us. She loves it. But she doesn't like us to be there too. She can't have her friends over to stay here, or go to them like other children. So having her own time with other children at the hospice is wonderful for her."

It is important to point out that the hospice provision accessed by the families we interviewed was run on a charitable basis and was not part of the multi-agency services. We were concerned to discover that for two families, the only short-breaks option available to them and their child was on a hospital ward.

A whole family approach to social well-being?

From the majority of families we spoke to, there was a very strong sense of their desire to do things together as a family unit, and to be viewed, as a *whole family*, not as a set of individuals with separate and non-convergent needs. Services often only cater either for the disabled child, or for siblings (occasionally), and it is therefore extremely difficult for carers to get a complete break, or do things together as a family. The lack of opportunities for families to do things together as a *normal* family and have time away from their responsibilities can lead to considerable emotional pressures being placed on the families.

Overall, the families we spoke to felt that little attention was paid to the *whole family* by the multi-agency services.

> "They all get together to discuss [child]. They don't talk about the rest of us much."

Several families were saddened that they could not go out together as a family unit, and there was a strong sense that all family members, but especially siblings, were missing out. For example, one mother talked of how her disabled child hated being out in the wind or rain and became very distressed. The boy's younger sibling found this very hard to understand and got very upset when told that they could not go out because of this.

Families talked frequently of the difficulties for siblings and the lack of support that was available for them. Only four families had access to, or had been offered access to, young carers or sibling groups. Seven families said that there was nothing available, with four of those explicitly stating that this was a problem. One family, with three children, two of whom (a girl, and a boy with complex health care needs) were fostered, explained that their birth child (a boy) did not get access to the same sort of holiday activities as the two foster children. He felt *left out*, particularly when the multi-agency service was offering exciting activities to his siblings, and missed the chance to spend time with his brother and sister in the school holidays.

There were some positive examples of support from multi-agency services to the family as a whole, such as a sitter being provided for a sibling while a nurse attended to the disabled child, half of childcare fees being paid for siblings while the disabled child was in hospital, a sibling attending a young carers' group, and a support worker was provided to one family to help with the care of siblings. Where a whole family approach to social well-being was evident, families felt that it:

> "Changes the whole outlook."

The impact that being supported to do things together had on the families of children with complex health care needs is highlighted by the following account from one father:

> "We went once to the ice rink and this young lad who works there came up to us and said if he got some blankets and put them on a sledge would we like to bring our son on the ice. It was the rarest of moments – all four of us together doing one thing. It made such a difference."

Emotional well-being

Past research has shown that the emotional component of support to families is very often overlooked by services (Kirk and Glendinning, 1999; Morris, 1999; Tozer, 1999; Kerr and Macintosh, 2000; Limbrick-Spencer, 2000). Although many parents may want emotional support, professionals may feel unwilling, or unable to give this, either because they feel it is outside of their role, or because parents tend to present problems of a more practical nature (Dobson and Middleton, 1998). Chamba et al (1999) found that Black and minority ethnic families were less likely to have support from their extended family than white families and that awareness and membership of support groups were low.

Sources of emotional pressure

Families caring for a child or young person with complex health care needs, experience considerable pressures in their daily lives, a large part of which is emotional strain. When talking to families, it became clear that there were common themes regarding the source of this emotional pressure.

Disagreements and lack of coordination between services

Where there was a lack of coordination among services it was in itself found to be a source of pressure:

> "The thing that drives me mad is that they [professionals] don't communicate with each other. Yes, it's very stressful and I'm on tablets for depression."

Several families talked about being exposed to disagreements between professionals from the multi-agency service about funding or financial aspects of service provision. Families found this distressing, inappropriate and disrespectful:

> "It was all about money and not how we were suffering as a family. I don't need to know the details of how budgets work, or to get involved in writing to different people. I don't care who pays as long as they pay."

Being on call 24 hours per day

Many families described the feeling of being *on call* 24 hours a day as a result of the need to both provide physical care, but also to be vigilant, in respect of their son or daughter's complex health care needs. Some families that we talked to described extremely distressing experiences, where their child had been near the point of death. Families talked about being very aware of choking, for example, and this led to a heightened sense of alert, with all its exhausting consequences on sleep and behaviour. Even when the child was at school, many parents were aware that they could be telephoned at any time to go to school to deal with a medical emergency with their child. In addition, some families reported that the frequent necessity of having to wait for equipment and supplies to be delivered was very restrictive. As one parent said:

> "Yes, I'm the lynchpin – if you took me out then it would collapse. Sometimes that's too much on me. I know he's my son but I feel it's my son with a whole other package with it."

Nursing tasks

The level of nursing care that the parents are providing to their children carries its own emotional pressure:

> "I don't have help with anything, just carry on with what we do ... I feel like a nurse sometimes. I don't feel like a mum anymore."

Several parents felt that this nursing role had been thrust upon them and that they had little choice about it if they wanted their child to be at home. One family, in particular, felt that once the child had come home from hospital, they had been forgotten by services and left to cope alone.

Lack of privacy

Families with disabled children are obliged to disclose an enormous amount of very personal information, sometimes to people that they do not know very well and this, to varying degrees, has a debilitating effect. They also talked of the intrusion into their homes by having carers for their child, with no control over *normal* things like when they got up or had meals. One family described their home as being like a railway station, with often no notice given of when professionals would turn up.

Lack of back-up and continuity

Several families mentioned the stresses involved in having no *back-up* cover if their child, or their child's usual (trained) carer, was ill. Many carers were only available to support the child at school, or during the school days. So, if the carer was ill, the child would have to remain at home. Or if the child was ill, the carer would have to remain in school, rather than be able to support the child at home. Obviously, having a child ill and off school is a difficult issue for many parents to contend with, particularly working parents. But it is even more difficult for families of children with complex health care needs as there is unlikely to be anyone else trained, or available, to look after their child.

Of those who had access to a named person or keyworker, it appeared that half of these families had received support from more than one keyworker throughout their involvement in the multi-agency service. In addition, families reported that when a keyworker left, or changed role, there had been a lack of clarity about ongoing coordinated support, which in some cases had caused a lot of difficulties. In one case, this meant that the family went without a keyworker for about six months and:

> "... then quite a few bits fell apart again."

Sources of emotional support for families

When asked about the emotional support that they received, nine families said that they had no emotional support whatsoever – neither from services, nor from wider family or friends. One parent held a view that was probably fairly universal among the families we spoke to, that of not wanting to be seen as a *problem* to people.

Asking for emotional support can be a very personal issue, and five families told us that they preferred to rely on family and friends. However, it was encouraging to note that half of the families who had access to a keyworker felt that, should they need it, this person would provide emotional support. In general, these seven families described a supportive, open relationship with their keyworker, suggesting that she or he could be contacted at any time in between scheduled meetings to discuss problems or issues.

> "She's a friendly face to talk to. I mean perhaps she doesn't know what it's like to have a disabled child, I don't know, but she's very supportive and I feel that I can actually open up to her quite easily so yes, she is very supportive."

> "I can say whatever I like to her, and I usually do, so yes that's emotionally very supportive."

Other families described access they had had to other professionals such as clinical psychologists, GPs, social workers, health visitors or nurses.

Support groups can play an important role in providing opportunities for parents and carers to discuss and share concerns and experiences. Sixteen families were involved in some sort of support group or network, ranging from informal support through the child's school to several families being matched with either individuals or groups via their coordinator. Five families reported that they would like this type of contact and a further two stated that they would like this but felt unable to because of the demands of caring for their child. There was evidence that families with a child with a rare condition did feel isolated, but some had used the Internet effectively to make contact with similar families either in the UK or in other countries.

Emotional support for children and young people with complex health care needs

Children and young people also need time and space to communicate their feelings and emotions (Beresford, 1997). And yet our interviews with families highlighted that there was very little emotional support offered to the disabled children and young people themselves. In fact, we only came across one instance of a child having access to this form of support, and when it did not work out, no alternative was offered. In another family, when the

father died, the siblings were offered bereavement counselling, but the disabled child was not, despite the fact that this child was expressing feelings of loss and distress. Although only a small number of parents (three) mentioned emotional support for the disabled child or young person as being needed, it does seem to be a significant gap in provision. Although there were examples of keyworkers making positive efforts to create relationships with the children they were linked to, it did not appear that this relationship extended to being a supportive one in the same way as it did for the children's parents.

Skills and learning

Access to education and learning opportunities for children and their parents is essential to a good quality of life. Previous research evidence suggests, however, that some children with complex health care needs are not able to access a full educational curriculum (Harvey, 1997; Noyes, 1999b; Townsley and Robinson, 2000; Mencap, 2001). Townsley and Robinson (2000) found that eight out of 38 families involved in their research study had experienced some difficulties in accessing education for their tube-fed child. Three of these children were not attending school at all. Where suitable provision is not available locally (due to lack of trained staff, or restrictive local policies), disabled children with complex health care needs may be offered a school place at some distance from their home, possibly at a residential school, with resulting social barriers (Abbott et al, 2001). Once young disabled people with complex health care needs reach the age of 19, there may not be adequate or appropriate provision available for them from adult services (Morris, 1999). Uncertainty about the future is a great source of worry for families of disabled children with complex health care needs (Townsley and Robinson, 2000).

Access to education for children and young people

In contrast to the findings of previous studies (Noyes, 1999b; Townsley and Robinson, 2000; Mencap, 2001) our interviews with families showed that all those children who were of school age were receiving education at a local school or nursery and were attending school on a regular basis (Table 8). It was very significant to discover that there was no evidence of major problems with access to education, and that children appeared to be very well supported during the school days.

> "He's got a one-to-one carer at school, a main carer plus he works with other adults, he's always got an adult with him."

> "She copes alright in mainstream school. She's got full-time support, but yes, she has done very well in school, far more than we ever, you know, dreamed of."

In general, families were very happy with their child's schooling and in most cases, the children were accessing the whole school curriculum.

> "School is the biggest source of support – they have such a positive attitude."

> "School is great. I'm confident about his well-being there."

There were a few exceptions to this, especially regarding swimming, physical education (PE), school trips and out-of-school activities. Six families stated that there was nothing available for disabled children in terms of out-of-school clubs or activities, or that their disabled child was not able to access what was available, in one instance because of transport difficulties. But overall, this picture is one in contrast to that described in earlier research into access to education for children with complex health care needs.

Interestingly, because representation from Education was largely missing from the six multi-agency teams or services we visited, the role played by the multi-agency service itself in terms of coordinating or facilitating access to education was fairly minimal. However, in two services, where the remit of the

Table 8: Type of school attended by children and young people

Type of school	Number of children
Special	7
Unit in mainstream	9
Mainstream	3
Too young for school or nursery	3
Special nursery	2
Not specified, but attending school	1

service was to provide children's medical and physical support via trained carers to enable them to live at home and to access school, this role was more expansive.

The coordination of learning support for disabled children with complex health care needs is certainly an area in which multi-agency services could usefully become involved. Liaison between Education and other agencies, such as Health, is likely to become increasingly significant as more children reach school age. Some thinking ahead, in terms of liaison between child and adults' services at transition and at age 19 would also be an area for fruitful input from multi-agency services.

Coordinating learning support outside school is another area that multi-agency services could consider. One family was very positive about their keyworker's efforts to secure funding for a computer for their son:

> "[Keyworker] is trying to help [child] get a computer … the way forward with him is to use a keyboard and get him really good on it, because by the time he is actually in school doing a lot of essay work, he is not going to be able to cope. If he is really good on the keyboard it is going to help him, so rather than doing it later, it is best off doing it now, so she is trying to sort that out, because that is quite a huge expense really."

Development of skills and learning for parents and carers

Supporting parents or carers to develop new skills in managing their child's complex health care needs at home was not an area that appeared to receive much attention from multi-agency services, once the child was back at home. Families told us that they received most, if not all, of their training from the hospital where their child's medical technology had been introduced. Seven families expressed a strong interest in more detailed input in this area and three families had even found out about appropriate courses for themselves, one of which was a postal course.

Learning more about how to communicate with their child was an area for training highlighted by several families. In service A, families had access to a well-established system of support and training on communication for disabled children and children with learning disabilities. But in other areas some families struggled to find out more about signing or other non-verbal communication techniques. For example, two of the families we spoke to explained how they had been very keen to learn more about how to communicate by signing with their disabled child, but that no support had been forthcoming. Consequently, both families looked into the issue themselves and arranged either to attend a local course, or to teach themselves.

> "I got no information when I asked so I just started going to a sign language course so I can learn to communicate with [child]."

> "We taught [child] to sign from about 5 months old. We did it all ourselves as she only had speech and language therapy twice in the first year of her life and this was for her feeding. We tried to find out about it, but no one helped us, so in the end we went on the Internet, bought some books and a video and taught ourselves. Now she's at school she's learnt 12 new signs in the last week."

Supporting parents to develop new skills in areas not specifically related to the care of their child is not generally an area that might be expected to fall within the remit of a multi-agency service. However, we did find evidence of several examples of unusual, and family-centred, learning support, as exemplified by the following quotes:

> "She helped me with driving ... because living in London, everything's on your doorstep anyway, tubes, buses, but down here we were saying about it and she actually got some help ... quite a lot of money for lessons."

> "I have met an awful lot of people through it so I think I've gained a lot of confidence going to different meetings, the coordination, we have got a meeting here, we have got a meeting here, we have got one coming up on February 8th ... so it has taught me an awful lot, definitely a lot more than I think I would have known otherwise."

The second of these quotes shows the important role that keyworkers can play as mentors, in terms of encouraging parents and carers to develop their confidence and skills in self-advocacy. The opportunity to develop a *supportive, open relationship* (Mukherjee et al, 1999) seems key in this respect.

Summary

- *Daily family life* – multi-agency services appeared to be providing effective, focused support to families in terms of managing their children's complex health care needs at home. In addition, the health needs of this group of children are largely well met except around some equipment and a lack of support when the child or young person first comes home from hospital. However, many of the families we interviewed had difficulties with daily routines, particularly sleeping, and there was no significant evidence that support from the multi-agency services (or from a keyworker) had enabled them to access more short breaks or sitting services to allow them *time out* from caring for their child 24 hours a day. Transport also continues to be a major problem for families and was not an area where advice or support was readily forthcoming from the multi-agency services.
- *Physical environment* – the majority of families we spoke to had made, or were planning, adaptations to their home. Although occupational therapists were cited as helpful during this process, very few families had received a coordinated response from the multi-agency service, even where there was evidence of access to a keyworker. Speedy adaptations can make a significant difference to families' quality of life, and in the absence of advice or funding support, some families had resorted to both organising and paying for their own adaptations.
- *Financial well-being* – three quarters of the families we interviewed had a gross family income that was below the national average. General help from multi-agency services with financial management was absent despite the fact that only two families said they had no concerns about money matters. Just under half of families had received support from the multi-agency services with claiming benefits entitlements. Employment of mothers (38%) was slightly higher than that of mothers of disabled children represented on the Family Fund database, whereas employment of fathers (58%) was largely similar to the Fund's figures.

Supporting families to find paid work could be facilitated through the coordination of more flexible and appropriate short breaks or sitting services.

- *Social well-being* – the families we interviewed all experienced major difficulties in finding and organising social activities for themselves and for their disabled children. The shortage of flexible, adequate and appropriate sitting or short-breaks services was thought to be responsible for this. The provision of flexible support that enables children and families to participate in a full range of social activities will very often mean support throughout the night, in the evenings, at weekends, on a 24-hour basis, and in an emergency. It did not appear that this level of support was an option for the families we interviewed, or that the six multi-agency services had the resources available to plan for, or offer, this degree of flexibility. The professionals supporting families appeared to be doing the best they could in the circumstances, but lack of resources left them powerless to provide for families' real needs in their area. Most families had a very strong desire to do things together and to be perceived as a *whole family*. Multi-agency services did not appear to be able to respond to this and the focus of support was very much focused on the disabled child with complex health care needs, to the detriment of other family members and the family unit as a whole.

- *Emotional well-being* – families reported numerous sources of emotional pressure, some of which were directly related to a lack of coordinated and flexible support from the multi-agency services. A large proportion of families felt they had no one to turn to for emotional support. However, nearly half of the families we spoke to felt confident that they could get support from the multi-agency service if they so wished and where this was offered it was highly valued by families. Support groups played an important role, but their existence was not widely known about by families, or publicised by services. Children and young people with complex health care needs were not given access to emotional support, despite a need for this being apparent. There is a real risk that children and families will suffer from mental distress where no emotional support is available. The negative impact of mental health problems on individual and family life cannot be overstated.

- *Skills and learning* – of those children who were of school age, all were attending a local school or nursery on a regular basis, and families expressed a high degree of satisfaction with the support and educational input their children received. The role of the multi-agency services in coordinating and facilitating access to education was fairly minimal, but potentially this could change if problems arise. Thus it seems important for multi-agency service providers, and keyworkers in particular, to develop and maintain good relationships with education professionals. Supporting parents and carers to develop new skills in managing their children's complex health care needs at home, or indeed in other areas such as communication, was not an area that appeared to receive much attention from the multi-agency services. However, several positive examples from families highlighted the important role that multi-agency professionals, such as keyworkers, can play in acting as mentors and encouraging parents and carers to develop their self-advocacy skills.

5

Exploring the impact of multi-agency working on families' contact with services and professionals

Past research (Mukherjee et al, 1999; Sloper, 1999; Tozer, 1999; Beattie, 2000) has highlighted that families want someone who can take an overview of their situation, who can put together a package of support, find solutions and understand the needs of the whole family. Parents also want flexibility in services so that spontaneity might be possible, a feature currently lacking in the lives of disabled children with complex health care needs.

As we saw in Chapter 2, all six of the multi-agency services we visited aimed to coordinate, standardise, clarify or simplify aspects of service provision for disabled children and their families. In addition, four of the sites had developed a multi-agency service that aimed to give families and children access to a keyworker to coordinate and facilitate their care and support. Even for the two sites where a keyworker was not an intrinsic part of service provision, these services aimed nonetheless to act as a central pivot, or point of contact for families and children. In addition, three services hoped that their form of multi-agency working would help to reduce duplication and minimise the numbers of appointments and professionals taking up the time of families.

Chapter 4 described the impact that multi-agency working had on families' daily lives. Chapter 5 now examines families' contact with professionals and agencies. Given that all six services aimed specifically to improve the nature of contact between professionals, agencies and families, what was the experience for families? How did families perceive the nature of their contact with the six services and

to what extent did it make a positive difference to their lives?

Access to services

We asked families if they thought it had been easier, or more difficult to get access to adequate support since their involvement in the multi-agency services. Twelve of the 25 families felt that access to services had been easier and seven said it was the same.

> "Easier, because I think they are more in contact with one another. Instead of saying we have got to wait for a report to come from so and so, it all seems to be glued together. I would say it's better."

> "It's the same. It's a step in the right direction but I haven't seen any obvious, visible differences to what we are getting yet. Nothing happens any faster. It's just the system."

Of the remaining families, two could not answer as they had always received the service (and thus had no point of comparison), two did not know and two families from one site said that access to services had been more difficult. Of the families that did not know, one of them stated that this was because they did not have a clear sense of what was available and what they could be getting.

Families gave some specific examples of the ways that sites had facilitated access to services:

> "Oh yes, they have been very good at getting, they got the eye appointment sorted out. Because I missed it

in May, I didn't mean to but I did, and I missed an eye appointment so I thought we would be struck off the clinic because we had missed it and I hadn't cancelled it. But [service coordinator] managed to get us another appointment."

Several families explained that the nature of a more coordinated, multi-agency approach meant that accessing services was indeed easier by virtue of the fact that more people were aware of, and responsible for, supporting them and their child.

"If we went to the [service] and [keyworker] wasn't there we'd be able to talk to someone else who would know about us and [child] and be able to help or give advice about who else to contact. And because they cross Health and Social Services, if there's a health problem they can deal with that too which is great."

There was also a small amount of evidence to suggest that access was improved as a result of contact with a keyworker whose role encompassed working together with families to establish their needs for services and support. Although not statistically significant as numbers are too small, when answers to the question about access to services were summed across sites, it appeared that the only two sites where access was mostly easier (as opposed to the same, worse, or unknown) were both sites providing keyworking.

Several families highlighted that *being a professional* was still the most effective way to get access to services, despite the rhetoric of *parent power*.

"Yes, even though they say parents have got the most power, you are so easily fobbed off, whereas a professional is not quite so, they can sort of stand up to them, you feel sometimes you mustn't argue with what that person has said, I am not saying [keyworker] will go out and argue with them but she can perhaps put it over in a different way than perhaps a parent can do."

From talking to families, it also emerged that the seniority of their keyworker was an issue when it came to access to services. Some families had access to keyworkers who were more senior professionals, or were indeed the manager of the service or project, and very much appreciated the added *clout* that this

seniority afforded them in terms of access to services. One family appreciated that the project manager had been involved at the start and *gelled it all together*, but they were concerned that their own keyworker did not have the same amount of influence.

Conversely, a few families had noticed that their keyworker was not perceived by other professionals as *powerful enough* to effect any changes for them and that this had an impact on their likely access to services:

"Particularly at the beginning when we were trying to get it all sorted out, [coordinator] was liasing with everybody and I think all the services were sympathetic, it was the purse-strings that were the problem."

Similarly, some families were aware of the inherent difficulties for those professionals (usually a keyworker) who were acting as advocates for families while also carrying out their own professionals duties as a social worker, therapist, nurse, and so on. Families understood how hard it was for these professionals, in particular, to advocate for things like equipment or funding when it was their own agency which was the provider of these things:

"They can't fight their own bosses."

Although we did not visit any sites where professionals were employed solely to be dedicated keyworkers, several families highlighted the importance of keyworkers being able to take a *service-neutral* approach to facilitating service provision:

"I consider the coordinators, because they are to me neutral people, I can say whatever I like to them, and I usually do."

Overall, however, there was an overriding concern from families that access to services was not necessarily an outcome of effective multi-agency working if professionals were simply coordinating existing (and inadequate) resources:

"The [multi-agency service] is really a very good move and has certainly improved things for me, but at the end of the day, it doesn't matter how many service coordinators you've got, [service] doesn't seem to have an awful lot of resources to meet the needs of these families. What's the point in them coming to sit in my lounge for an hour and sort of say lets put the world to rights, when they are powerless to do anything about it anyway, which is not their fault?"

Coordination of services

All of the six multi-agency services had a remit to coordinate services for families of disabled children with complex health care needs. Four of the six multi-agency services had established a clear model of *service coordination*, which included access by families to a named person known variously as a keyworker, service coordinator or link worker (throughout this report we have used the term, keyworker as a generic term for this role). Our interviews with families revealed that 13 of the 15 families included in the research from these four sites had access to a keyworker. For the 10 families interviewed from the remaining two sites, coordination of services was less formally organised, and families were less clear about whether or not one named person undertook this role for them.

Despite the differences in approach across the six sites, a distinct lack of clarity about the role of a keyworker emerged, particularly in terms of the very nub of what they were supposed to do – coordinate services for families. Indeed, of the 25 families we interviewed, only six felt that their keyworker (or the multi-agency service) did actually coordinate services for them, and two of these families said the effectiveness of this was variable. On the other hand, four families explicitly said that despite a commitment towards coordination by the multi-agency service with which they were in contact, they still did all the coordinating themselves:

"There's no chance of ever getting that [coordination]! Who could do it as well as me, who'd know how everything fitted together for [child]? Services are too fragmented and too scattered around. [Multi-agency service] is brilliant, but we have to mediate between them all."

"It's a good idea [coordination]. I spend a lot of time on the 'phone sorting things out. It's very tiring and sometimes you just give up because it doesn't seem worth the effort. No one's talked to me about this."

For those families who did have access to a keyworker, various issues were raised in relation to the effectiveness of this role. For example, a high staff turnover in some areas was problematic for maintaining continuity. Seven families had been in contact with more than one keyworker since their involvement in the multi-agency service had begun. In some cases this had been because of staff leaving, meaning that families had periods where they did not have a keyworker. There were examples of difficulties arising because of this:

"Because she [keyworker] had been in regular contact and a lot of the problems I had, if she had been there, I would have just got on to her to sort out. As it was, things just fell apart again."

Ineffectiveness of the keyworking role also included families feeling they had been *let down* by keyworkers, or that they still had to say things over and over again and that messages did not get passed on.

On the positive side, however, many families appreciated the time and effort that went into coordinating services and were pleased to have some of the burden lifted from them:

"I was spending so much time on the 'phone, I would be chasing up changed appointments ... so yes, that's cut down on oodles of 'phone calls."

Families recognised that their keyworkers had specific skills and knowledge that they did not necessarily possess and were able to choose when to ask them to take on tasks that they knew would be difficult for them:

"Sometimes you just don't know who you need to talk to, so I speak to the service coordinator and she puts me in touch with the right person. But most of the time she takes over, or if I want her to, and then takes it from there."

Families appreciated the help that their keyworkers gave them in relation to meetings – help with the preparation of reports, getting professionals together and *guiding* the family through the ways in which the service worked.

"She sets up everything, makes sure everything is happening. I ring her if I have any problems. All the equipment I need and that she organises and she makes sure that everybody else is doing their job properly."

The families reported some instances of keyworkers going *above and beyond* duties. Some keyworkers made a positive effort to get to know the child with complex health care needs and other members of the family, and this was very much appreciated. Five keyworkers were found to have made specific contact with the child with complex health care needs and in four further cases other people from the multi-agency initiative had regular contact. Where it existed, families very much appreciated this *whole family* approach to keyworking:

"I know she keeps the whole team informed about our family's needs. It's lovely to have a team who works as a whole. In other places they work as individuals. If we went to the team and our coordinator wasn't there we'd be able to talk to someone else who would know us and our son and be able to give advice and help about who to contact."

Providing a single point of contact

The four sites that put families in touch with a keyworker did so in order, partly, to provide a single pathway, or point of contact for accessing the service. The other two sites also believed that, as a service, they acted as a central pivot, or point of contact for families and children. As we saw in Chapter 1, however complex the workings of a partnership might be *behind the scenes*, people using the service should be able to understand and to access the process easily, preferably via a single point of contact (Sloper, 1999; Interconnections, 2001).

Initial access to the multi-agency service was usually via some sort of referral and assessment process. It was sometime later that most families were matched with a keyworker, where appropriate. Chapter 2 has already highlighted that there was some confusion and disagreement among professionals about issues such as eligibility criteria, referral, assessment, and nature and regularity of reviews. Professionals had also voiced concerns about duplication of assessment and reviews across agencies, even where a multi-agency approach had been agreed. Each of the six

multi-agency services carried out an assessment of child and family need, which involved a range of professionals. This usually formed the basis of a care plan. However, some agencies still carried out their own additional assessments and did not routinely involve other professionals or agencies.

Families' experiences of the multi-agency assessment process

Our interviews with families echoed the findings from professionals. The families reported that their needs were assessed in most cases in multidisciplinary meetings. Thirteen families talked of a large meeting with several professionals from different agencies being present, three families had had meetings in hospital while their child was still a patient and one talked of an assessment being carried out at the child's school. With the remaining families, meetings had been carried out individually with either the project manager, the keyworker, an occupational therapist, or in one case the keyworker and a carer who had been employed to help the family.

Concerns were expressed by some of the families who had had a multi-agency meeting to assess needs. One family reported that 25 professionals were at the meeting and it had been *very scary*. Two families felt that the meeting had not been helpful and one said that it was just to work out who was going to pay for services. One family did not like the formality of the meeting and had the feeling that they had been talked about before they went in. The parents also did not like the fact that several of the people in the meeting did not know the child or themselves:

"It is big tables and business-like, but it's not business-like to me, it's my child and I'd be happier sitting on the floor ... I got my hair done and a suit for the first time I went."

Some families were still finding that there was a high degree of duplication regarding assessments:

"Everyone came together to do the Care Plan, but the Social Services plan is different from the Education plan and then there's a separate plan for Health. At the hospital there was different meetings and different plans. There's a plan, for example, about the shared care that she gets."

And some families had chosen to have the assessments combined with, for example, education reviews to cut down on the number of meetings that they were required to attend.

Families' experiences of the multi-agency review process

Reviewing the needs of families is an important part of multi-agency service provision, and one would expect that the multi-agency service would play a central role in planning and facilitating this process, particularly where families were matched with a keyworker whose role it was to act as a single point of contact.

Of the 25 families interviewed, only seven believed that their needs were reviewed regularly by the multi-agency service in which they were involved. On further analysis, it became clear that most families *were* having their needs reviewed, but in sometimes very informal and unclear ways, and not always via the multi-agency services themselves. For example, families reported that they had been involved in reviews led and coordinated by Education, by a joint review between Education and the multi-agency service, informally with their coordinator, by 'phone with the multi-agency manager or via the foster care service. Two families said that they had numerous reviews, including one with the multi-agency service. Three families did not know how their needs were reviewed.

Some families were concerned that commitment to review meetings dropped off after a while. This drop-off in commitment was shown by the fact that the more senior professionals stopped coming after a few meetings where there had been initial enthusiasm. This is a concern which is related to the earlier point made about the difficulties for less senior professionals to have the power to make decisions, especially around funding. If the professionals who can make decisions about funding and services are not present at review meetings, it slows down the process, and causes delays and uncertainty for families.

The role of a named person or coordinator as a single point of contact

It is clear that even where families had access to a keyworker that this fact alone did not have a significantly positive impact on their experience of the assessment and review process. However, contact with a keyworker provided a single point of contact for some families in other, more positive, ways. For example, several families appreciated the fact that they could now route any enquiry via just one person, as opposed to trawling round professionals until they found the right person to deal with their query.

"Well, I think [keyworker] will know everything and you can go to just the one person."

"I know if I want to get hold of anybody I can always 'phone her ... it's one 'phone call for me instead of 10 trying to get through to the right person."

Communication between families and professionals

Chapter 1 highlighted the importance of multi-agency services finding a clear way to communicate regularly with children and families. Regular, open communication can help to create a culture of trust, respect and honesty. Common assessment tools and arrangements for shared access to records can help to avoid miscommunication between professionals themselves and between professionals and families. It is obvious that professionals should provide good quality information and advice to families and children. However, families and children also have important insights and advice to offer professionals. Communication thus involves the two key elements of information provision and consultation.

Information and advice

Disabled children, young people and their families need access to good quality information and regular, accurate advice in order to feel empowered and to control and manage their situation. And yet previous research has suggested that many families and children neither get the information they need, nor are satisfied with its quality and quantity. Mitchell and Sloper (2000) found that families valued information that was available in both summary and more detailed formats, and was supplemented by direct, personal contact with a keyworker or other professional. Mitchell and Sloper found that families wanted direct contact with a person who could guide them through the maze of potentially useful and available information. They also valued continuity, time to share information and the recognition that professionals should share information across agencies. The value of shared information and records is even more important for families of children with complex health care needs who are likely to be in contact with many different professionals and agencies. Hand-held records, or a well-designed database, are key tools in this respect (Mukherjee et al, 2000).

The frequency with which the families we interviewed had contact with the multi-agency service varied widely. Most families and children had some regular contact with therapists at home or at school. But in terms of access to a keyworker, some families described regular, scheduled meetings (every two to three months) alongside more responsive ad hoc support ('phone calls, extra home visits), whereas other families only had contact with their coordinator in an emergency or at a review meeting. There was no consistency about frequency of contact within or between the six multi-agency services. This can partly be explained by family preferences about contact, although there was evidence that in some cases, the families would have liked more contact.

These findings also raise the question of whether the multi-agency services, or keyworkers in particular were providing *proactive, regular contact*, a prerequisite for good communication between families and professionals (Mukherjee et al, 2000).

"I would like to see him popping into the house to check everything's OK, or if there's anything we need, but he doesn't do that."

Contact was primarily between the main carers (mostly mothers) and services. Over half of the families we visited felt that the needs of their child were considered first, rather than the needs of the whole family. Only two families said that their keyworker had contact with members of the family

other than the main carer and the child with complex health care needs. A further two families said that they had contact *in passing*. As mentioned in Chapter 5, many families thought that the multi-agency services should pay more attention to the whole family, with most comments relating to siblings whom the families felt suffered as a result of all the attention and services being focused on the child with complex health care needs.

In one service, a keyworker suggested that the structure of the service and meetings had kept both mothers and fathers involved in the life of their child. It actively promoted fathers being involved and also kept parents who had separated working together in the best interests of their child. When asking families if they thought that the whole family was helped by the project or service, only three families agreed, with a further three saying that the whole family was helped to a certain extent, but not fully. The research shows that there is a clear need for services and projects to take an holistic approach and to consider the needs of the whole family. Without this, it cannot truly be said that families are supported in a way that is beneficial or will have long-term outcomes.

There was a mixed response from the families regarding access to the records that are kept about their children. Hand-held records are a file or folder that the families keep at home, which they and professionals across agencies add to. Although interviews with families appeared to indicate that hand-held records were available, informally, at several sites, the nature of these was not entirely clear, and their existence was not corroborated by evidence from interviews with professionals. There was only one site that had formally introduced the notion of hand-held records, in the format of a 'blue bag'.

"We have got hand-held records, to be filed we keep it together which is useful for people like me. So if I get a letter now, I just pop it straight in my blue bag and then at some point when I've got a minute, I can consolidate it and check back. It's got a calendar bit, which is useful. And [keyworker] is going to come round and we are going to run down and get it together and sort it and update the information."

Of the families that did have this type of record, several families were very positive about this.

However, others expressed concern that busy professionals would not find the time to add to them.

"I was wondering if I put this under the consultant's nose would he take the time to write in it, because a lot of people probably wouldn't want to."

A further seven families did have copies of reports and notes from meetings sent to them, although there was no system of adding to these themselves. Several professionals talked about problems of confidentiality in terms of sharing records between agencies. Interestingly, this was not an issue that was raised by any of the families we spoke to.

Consultation with families

Listening to the views and experiences of families and children, and acting on their insights is an essential component of effective support. Many families have developed extensive knowledge and expertise of their child's specific health care needs. In addition, children and young people will have their own views about their care and support (Shakespeare et al, 1999) – we will discuss communication between professionals and children/young people in Chapter 6. Townsley and Robinson (2000) found that where families' views were valued, they felt that they had more control over decisions about their child's health, and the technological intervention itself was likely to be perceived more positively.

Families were asked how well they thought professionals listened to them and took account of their views. Seventeen of the 25 families felt that they were listened to, with three of those saying that they 'mostly' felt listened to, but not all the time. Similarly, 20 of the 25 families thought that the professionals they had contact with did respect their views.

"They treat us as fellow professionals."

Four families thought that they were not listened to at all and these same four families also felt that their views were not respected. These four families were involved in different multi-agency services, so this finding cannot be attributed to a certain model of multi-agency work, but rather to the demands of their keyworker's job, the keyworker's personality and/or that of their own.

Chapter 2 looked at the process of family involvement in planning, developing and evaluating services from the perspective of professionals. The interviews with professionals suggested that three of the multi-agency services had developed pathways for regular consultation with families, whereas in the other three services there was little evidence of partnership, although these sites recognised that more work was needed in this area. Families' views largely concurred with these findings; regular and formalised partnership and consultation were rare and practice was patchy and lacked clarity of purpose to the families who took part. Several families mentioned that they had been involved in consultations for different aspects of the multi-agency services, but that they were unaware of what use had been made of their views, if anything.

Families' views of the overall impact of multi-agency working on their quality of life

We asked families if they felt that, overall, their involvement in the multi-agency services had improved the quality of their lives. Of the 25 families interviewed, 16 said that 'yes, family quality of life had improved overall'. Despite the many problems and difficulties faced by families, it is interesting that so many responded positively. The ways in which families said their lives had improved included not having to go into school with their child every day, getting more sleep and a reduction in the number of appointments they had to attend.

Although two families were not able to answer this question, only one thought that their life was worse and this was related to a worsening of their child's condition over this period. It is probably more significant to note that six families believed that the multi-agency service had not made any difference to their quality of life overall.

"It's a step in the right direction but good things have stayed good and bad things have stayed bad."

Although not statistically significant, because numbers are too small, it is interesting to note that when answers to the question about impact on quality of life were summed up across sites, it appeared that those sites where most families reported that their quality of life was mostly better (as opposed to the same, worse or unknown) were all sites where families had access to a keyworker to coordinate their services and support.

Summary

- *Access to services* – half of the families we interviewed felt that their access to support had improved since their involvement in the multi-agency service. Although only two families thought that access to services had been more difficult, the large number of families (more than a quarter of those interviewed) who felt that access was the same is an issue that warrants some attention. It emerged that families believed the seniority of their keyworker was significant in terms of facilitating access to services. They were also aware of the difficulties inherent in a role that combined family advocacy with representing a particular agency in a different capacity (for example as a therapist, social worker, and so on). Families also pointed out that the basic problem of inadequate provision of services in many areas reduced the benefits of attempts to improve access through a more coordinated approach.

- *Coordination of services* – over half of the families we interviewed had access to a keyworker with a specific remit to coordinate services for them. Despite this, there was a distinct lack of clarity regarding the role of this person, and only six out of the 25 families felt that the keyworker or the multi-agency service did actually coordinate services for them. Consequently, it appeared that families were still doing a lot of coordination themselves and that this was an area of quality of life where multi-agency services had not made great headway in supporting families.

- *Providing a single point of contact* – many of the families we interviewed were still experiencing multiple assessments and reviews, not something that goes in tandem with attempts to provide a single point of contact for access to multi-agency services. Families did not appear to have access to regular reviews of their needs or to have a clear picture of their entitlements. The presence of a keyworker did not seem to have a significant

impact on families' experiences of duplication in assessment and review; however, this person did provide a single point of contact in other, more positive ways.

- *Communication between families and professionals* – the frequency and regularity of contact between families and professionals varied greatly and seemed largely dependent on individuals' circumstances rather than the result of a particular service model. Findings from families did not appear to show significant evidence of *proactive, regular* contact from professionals. Nor did there seem to be much evidence of a whole family approach – rather the mother was the main focus for contact, with siblings and other family members being marginalised by multi-agency services. Some families expressed ambivalence about the status and usefulness of hand-held records and whether these would be used and valued by the professionals with whom they were in contact. Families were generally positive about the experience of being listened to, and having their views valued by professionals from the six multi-agency services. But family involvement in planning, developing and evaluating services was fairly ad hoc and lacked clarity of purpose to the families who did take part.

- *Overall impact on quality of life* – two thirds of the families we interviewed reported that the multi-agency service had made a positive difference to the overall quality of their lives. It is worth highlighting, however, that nearly a quarter of the families we spoke to felt that their involvement in the multi-agency service had made no discernable difference to their quality of life. It was not clear how much impact multi-agency working had made on disabled children and young people and this is a question to which we shall now turn in Chapter 6.

6

How do disabled children and young people with complex health care needs experience multi-agency working?

Disabled children and young people have their own observations about the services and support they receive. Although the importance of communicating directly with disabled children and young people is now widely acknowledged (Cigno and Gore, 1999) and supported by the legislation (1989 Children Act; 1995 Children [Northern Ireland] Order; 1995 Children]Scotland] Act), it is still relatively rare for this to happen in practice (Beresford, 1997; Kelly et al, 2000). But as Shakespeare et al (1999) point out, listening to children leads to a much richer understanding of their needs.

With this in mind, we were very keen that the thoughts and views of disabled children and young people with complex health care needs should be sought directly, and separately from those of their parents, carers and the professionals with whom they were in contact. This chapter examines in more detail the experience of multi-agency working from the perspective of those disabled children with complex health care needs involved in the six multi-agency services we visited.

Spending time with disabled children and young people with complex health care needs

Many, but not all, disabled children with complex health care needs are likely to have high-support needs and communication impairments. Some children may communicate non-verbally via body movements, or non-linguistic sounds. Other children may communicate through language via a communication board or computerised communication device. Potter and Whittaker (2001) explored how to create enabling communication environments for children with minimal or no speech. They highlighted a range of communication-enabling strategies for teachers and other professionals that included giving children time to communicate and reducing the amount of speech used by adults. Work by Triangle (2001) and the Children's Society (2001) showed that all disabled children can be included and enabled to express their wishes and feelings, but that sensitivity, time and a willingness to try a range of approaches were required. Disabled children involved in the work carried out by Triangle (2001) felt that adults who did not listen and did not try to communicate 'on all channels' created the real barrier to communication.

We were very aware of the need to be open to children's individual communication needs, and were mindful of the fact that in the past, disabled children with complex health care needs have often been excluded from research, due to the nature of their communication impairments and high-support needs. We were also aware that families very often feel concerned about the prospect of a *stranger* (in this case a researcher) attempting to communicate with their child about what appears to be a very abstract process (in this case, multi-agency working).

We thus developed a methodology for consulting with children and young people that was designed to be as child-centred, and non-intrusive as possible. We wanted to reassure parents and carers that we would be sensitive to their own knowledge and experience regarding the communication needs of their child, while trying as far as possible to value the importance of gaining a real picture of the child's own experiences from his or her point of view. Given the time and budgetary constraints of the research project, we were only able to visit a family and child once. We knew, therefore, that for many children, their parent or carer would need to be present to act as an interpreter or *proxy* throughout the communication process.

We approached children and young people via their primary carer, at home. We produced a pictorial leaflet/consent form with a photograph of the researcher who would be visiting the child, to explain the purpose of the visit and to ask for the child's consent to take part in the research. We were under no illusion that for the majority of children, their primary carer would be acting as an intermediary during the consent process, and although this presented some ethical dilemmas in terms of informed consent, it was a necessary part of attempting to gain access to this group of children.

This process was very successful in terms of recruiting children and young people to the project. Parents were generally very pleased that their children were being included, and were very keen to help in whatever way they could. This was reflected by the fact that out of the 25 families, consent was given for time to be spent with 18 of the children and young people. Given that all of these children and young people had high-support needs and communication impairments (as well as complex health care needs), and that one child was in hospital, we were very happy to receive such a high response rate. As with families (see Chapter 1), the children and young people who participated in the research did so on a self-selecting basis, and we were thus unable to sample by age, sex or ethnic identity. However, the children and young people who we did spend time with were fairly representative of the group as a whole, as discussed under the heading of 'The children and young people', to be discussed later.

Time was spent with the children and young people in their own homes, almost always with a parent or carer present, but in one case the child was seen at school with his support worker. The sessions lasted for about an hour, were informal and adapted to meet the needs of each individual child or young person. In some instances the child drew on large sheets of paper, sometimes the interviewer did. The sessions were designed to be as relaxed and enjoyable as possible, and with the parent's consent, the children were given a small gift and a £10 voucher for taking part.

We used a topic guide as the basis for gaining a picture of children and young people's experiences of multi-agency working. The guide covered the following areas: things I like; things I don't like; who lives at home with me; school; friends; adults who help me; short breaks; things that are difficult to do; and general happiness. Where appropriate, the children and young people were asked about what they thought about seeing so many professionals. They were also asked whether or not they had, or were aware of having, a keyworker.

The boxed example is an illustrative example of the kind of session where members of the research team spent time with disabled children and young people to find out more about their experiences of multi-agency working. The name of the child in the example has been changed.

The children and young people

Time was spent with 18 children and young people. Their ages ranged from between two years old to 15 years old (Table 9).

There were 11 boys (61%) and 7 girls (39%). This reflects the general population of disabled children across the six sites, drawing on data from the Family Fund's database, where it was found that 62% were boys and 38% were girls. Ten of the children and young people had no verbal communication, some of them used signs, a further three had limited verbal communication and used some signs as well. The remaining five did have some verbal communication. All the children and young people were dependent

Table 9: Ages of the children and young people we spent time with

Age	Number of children and young people (18)
0 to 3 years	2
4 to 7 years	8
8 to 11 years	6
12 to 15 years	2
Over 16 years	0

Spending time with Diana – by Debby Watson, researcher

The interview was held in Diana's own home, and I was helped by her adoptive mother. Diana is eight years old and has no verbal communication, but uses a communication book and some signs. She has a very close relationship with her mother, who has cared for her since 1995.

Diana has cerebral palsy, epilepsy and a gastrostomy. She frequently needs suction to prevent her from choking and she is in a wheelchair with head support. She is able, with difficulty, to move her head to look at her communication book, can smile and can move her arms to make approximate signs. It requires a great deal of patience and sensitivity to be able to understand her communication style.

I used large sheets of paper to write down what Diana was communicating to me and showed her what I had put down. Her understanding of this appeared to be fairly good. The interview was tape-recorded, with her consent.

Family
We started off by talking about Diana's family. She lives with her mother and wanted her granddad and nanny to be written down as important family people. She also wanted the names of three of her rabbits to be written down.

School
We then moved on to school, and I used another sheet to write down who was important to Diana. We established that she had a 'circle of friends' consisting of four children and she wanted another friend's name to be added to this list as well. She made clear choices about who to include. We then talked about all the adults who Diana saw at school, and this amounted to 10 people. They included her main teacher, three learning support workers, a physiotherapist, a speech and language therapist, an occupational therapist and a specialist teacher for children with hearing and sight impairments.

Activities
Next I established what Diana liked doing. The activities included cooking, shopping, going in the garden on her 'whizzy bike', listening to stories, watching television, swimming, going to the park, playing with her animals, bowling and Brownies. I attempted to ask Diana if there was anything that she would like to do that she was not able to at the moment. This proved a bit too challenging and Diana actually fell sleep at this point, but it was interesting that her mother pointed out that although Diana does do many activities, this is only really possible because she herself goes with Diana to support her. For example, the school takes the children swimming, but her mother has to go with Diana because no one is willing to take the risk of Diana choking in the pool. She questioned how inclusive services, especially education, really were.

Support at home
The final piece of work that we did was about people that Diana sees at home. She sees a total of eight people who help with her care. She has two night carers, one home help, someone who irons her clothes, a daytime carer, a social worker and an occupational therapist. We established that it was her night carers, the home help and her daytime carer that were especially important to her. Through using her communication book, and by asking what she thought about *all these people* who come to see her, Diana was able to sign that she thought it was both *silly* and *boring* to have to see so many people. Through using her communication book we also established that she was generally a happy person.

Diana was very tired by the time we had reached this point. We had been talking for an hour and both her mother and I felt that Diana had worked very hard and given us a lot of very useful information. Diana's mother was very happy with what we had achieved and was pleased that Diana had been consulted.

Table 10: Type of medical technology used by the children and young people we spent time with

Type of technology	Number of children (18)
Tube-fed	17
Suction	9
Oxygen	3
Catheter	2
Tracheotomy	3
Humidifier	1
Nebuliser	1
Cardiorespiratory monitoring	1

on medical technology; mostly the children were tube-fed and on suction (Table 10).

Families

Most of the children and young people lived with their birth parents. Two children lived with foster parents, a single mother adopted one and one lived with grandparents. All but four of the children and young people had siblings living at home with them. In the time spent with the children and young people, the importance of close physical contact, especially with mothers, was very apparent. Several children and young people liked cuddles with them, and others mentioned reading together and whispering. Nearly all the families had pets, which were also important to the children. Some of the children had close relationships with grandparents and other extended family members, but one mother reported that it saddened her that her extended family did not take the trouble to get to know how to communicate with her son.

Friendships

As can be seen from the table below, the children with verbal communication had the highest number of friendships (Table 11). It is also encouraging to see that a reasonable number of children with little or no verbal communication also had friends. The detail of these relationships is not very clear, although at least two children and young people did mention having friends round to their house to play or listen to music.

Professionals

The children and young people, where possible, were asked what they thought about the professionals in their lives. The most common response was that the children coped well with seeing different professionals, but it did make a real difference if the professionals made an effort to talk to the children and young people directly. There were special relationships mentioned with carers, especially where the children had short breaks. Parents reported that children needed time to get to know new people and relax with them. One child, whose experience was described in the boxed example above, used a communication board and indicated that she thought it was both *silly* and *boring* to see so many professionals. She did have a particularly high number of professionals in her life, seeing 10 different professionals at school and eight at home who were involved in her care.

One child talked of his care in hospital as being very difficult:

"Being in hospital is quite horrible really. I do get to meet new friends and talk to other parents but sometimes I don't like the way they talk to me. I went to get a towel and you're allowed but the man said, 'what are you doing here, you're always in my way, get back to bed'. I felt like he shouldn't have talked to me like that.... One woman really forced my line once and it hurt ... made me feel dizzy. I'm always

Table 11: Type of friendships experienced by the children and young people we spent time with

Type of friendship	Number of children with verbal communication	Number of children without any, or with very limited, verbal communication
Several friends	4	3
Friends aided by teacher		3
No real friends		1
Not aware of other children		1
One friend	1	2
Missing data		3

getting asked, 'What drugs are you on, what feeds are you on?' and so on ... it's so boring."

There was no evidence that the children and young people were given any choices about who helped with their care, although one young man said he preferred male carers.

Relationship with keyworker

Only one parent, talking about their child's relationship with their keyworker, spoke of them being very attached to the child and cited examples of the keyworker bringing him special things, which she knew he would like. The child in this case knew and recognised the keyworker. Two children very definitely did not know their keyworker; one parent said that the keyworker took no time to communicate with her child when she came to visit; another had only met the keyworker twice, but knew other professionals from the service quite well. One of the children said of her keyworker:

"She doesn't help me, she talks to me!"

This child was differentiating between her helper at school who enabled her to take part in all aspects of the school curriculum and whom she was very fond of, and the keyworker who came to visit and talk to her.

The general lack of contact that keyworkers had with the children and young people is therefore very apparent, as the remaining children and young people made no mention of them as being part of their lives. As we have seen from the evidence from professionals, some would like to have this relationship with the children and young people, but felt constrained within their roles to make this happen.

School

All the children and young people that we spent time with, except for one child who was too young (aged 2) were in full-time education, as shown in Table 12.

This, as has already been mentioned in Chapter 5, is a very encouraging picture. One of the multi-agency

Table 12: Type of school attended by the children and young people we spent time with

Type of school	Number of children and young people
Mainstream primary school	4
Mainstream secondary school	1
Unit in mainstream primary school	4
Special school	6
Special nursery	2

services that helped children with the highest number of medical technologies, specifically employed carers to enable children to attend school.

Adult helpers at school

The range of people that the children and young people saw at school ranged from one child who was reluctant to make contact with anyone at school, even his teacher, to another child who had contact with a large number of adult helpers and professionals. Most children saw at least three adults in school regularly. Several children had very close relationships with their helpers at school, with one child saying that she:

"Looks after me and keeps me safe."

Access to full curriculum

Generally, the children seemed to be happy with school life and were able to access most areas of the curriculum. However, there were some things that the children and young people could not do as a result of their complex health care needs, and this was a concern to some:

"I can't do PE at school, which is horrible really. If I didn't have my line in I could do it. My mates understand, I told some of them about it and my teacher told some of them."

There were four children who were unable to go swimming or to hydrotherapy with their school. In two cases, this was because of the MRSA bug, another child could not go since having a tracheotomy because the school were unhappy about the risk, and another child could only go swimming if the mother accompanied her, again because of the risk involved. This was important to the children and parents.

Things the children and young people liked

The children and young people liked a wide range of things, too many to list individually, but they included the following:

- going bowling
- pets/animals
- music
- videos
- swimming/hydrotherapy
- cuddles/strokes
- playing board games/jigsaws
- shopping
- going to the park
- being outside/playing in the garden
- painting/drawing/colouring
- TV
- having a bath/shower/Jacuzzi
- musical toys
- lights/sensory room
- brightly coloured or special toys
- playing with friends
- clean nappies
- being with people/voices.

When asked if it was easy to do these things, it was clear on several occasions that the children and young people needed considerable support to do them. This, to a certain extent, would generally be the case for most children, but with non-disabled children it would only be the case for a few years, after which they could hope to become more independent. One parent voiced this concern for children with complex health care needs:

"[Child] needs to have some independence, away from us. This is really difficult, because we have to find someone to be with her who we trust and who is trained. How can children with complex health care needs have independence as young people, away from adults?"

Other things that the children identified that they were not able to do were:

- go out with friends after school (because of being on a machine);
- go to an after-school club (because of over-tiredness);
- dress themselves;
- have a computer at home (too expensive);
- have a bath at home (no adaptation to ground floor to accommodate a bathroom);
- walk (but hoping to soon);
- go down a slide or play with paint (because of skin condition).

Things that the children and young people did not like

The children were able to identify 25 different things that they did not like, and a very high proportion of these (14) were related either to medical or physical issues. They included:

- being in hospital;
- not being able to do a certain physical activity;
- no play leader in hospital;
- being on a machine;
- "Things that the doctor does to me" (that is injections, bursting blisters);
- having a dirty nappy;
- suction;
- feeling unwell;
- feeling uncomfortable;
- anaesthetic;
- wearing splints.

Other things that the children and young people did not like included:

- noise
- shops
- wind and rain in face
- being told off
- feeling left out
- teasing.

Given the complex health care needs of these children, it is perhaps not surprising that so many of them mentioned issues relating to physical discomfort. This is where their experiences differ from those of other children. Their experiences of feeling left out and being teased would fit into a more general picture of the experiences of disabled children described in the literature. It would be interesting to discover how far having a keyworker who was interested and connected specifically with the child or young person would go to making life better in this respect. Also, the lack of emotional support that was identified in Chapter 5 could be of significance here.

General well-being

The children and young people were asked, where possible, to indicate if they were generally happy, sad or in-between by pointing to a range of faces on a sheet of paper. Where this was not possible, parents were asked to do this on their behalf. In most cases, the children and young people were either happy or contented most of the time, the exception to this being two children who indicated that they were not happy when they were in hospital. There was only one young person who indicated that he was very unhappy.

The children and young people described themselves (or were described) as:

- amenable, easily won over;
- contented generally, but unhappy in hospital;
- generally a bit depressed, hates hospital;
- happy, smiley, sociable;
- happy, sometimes giggly, sometimes whingey;
- content, makes happy sounds;
- smiley, mischievous, not often upset;
- generally happy;
- contented;
- smiley usually, sometimes neutral;
- very content;
- very content and happy;
- very happy;
- mixed – sometimes happy, sometimes unhappy.

What do these findings tell us about how disabled children and young people experience multi-agency working?

The support necessary to enable children and young people with complex health care needs to have an ordinary, happy life is not a luxury, but a basic human

right. It is clear that these children and young people wanted what any young person would want – friends, opportunities to interact with other people of their own age, and to be treated with respect and dignity.

The time we spent with children and young people, however, demonstrated that despite good intentions by the six multi-agency services, this group of children were still experiencing multiple barriers to exercising some basic human rights.

Right to communicate

More than half of the disabled children and young people with whom we spent time had no verbal communication. Some of these children used signs, but not all had a recognised, individualised means of communicating with others. In Chapter 4, we saw that several families were keen to support their child to develop a communication system, but that some had found it difficult to receive prompt, appropriate help from the multi-agency service with this. Families talked about a lack of emotional support for children with complex health care needs, and the time spent with children and young people highlighted that there are few, if any, outlets or opportunities for this group to describe and express the pain, discomfort and distress that they experience as a result of their need for complex health care interventions.

Article 10 of the 1998 Human Rights Act enshrines the right to freedom of expression. And the UN Convention on the Rights of the Child (1989, Article 13) sets out all children's rights to freedom of expression, including the freedom to seek, receive and impart information and ideas of all kinds, regardless of barriers, either orally, in writing or in print, in the form of art, or through any other media of the child's choice.

Right to independence

The vast majority of children and young people we spent time with had close, but extremely dependent relationships with their parents or carers. Children and young people were reliant on their family, and other adult carers, not only to support them with their complex health care needs and personal care, but also to support them in every other area of their lives. Very few children and young people could spend time alone with friends, or begin to develop some independence away from close family members. One or two families (quoted in Chapter 4) talked about how they were trying to find ways to support their children with complex health care needs to have more independence, but admittedly this was a very difficult area for parents and carers to consider, given the degree of their involvement with their child's daily care and support.

Recent policy initiatives in England, Wales and Scotland focusing on people with learning disabilities and disabled children and young people ('Valuing People' white paper [DoH, 2001a]; 'Fulfilling the promises' proposals framework [Learning Disability Advisory Group, 2001]; 'The same as you?' review of services [Scottish Executive, 2000]) set out the key principle of independence and urges public services to provide the support needed to maximise this. They also highlight that independence in this context does not mean doing everything unaided. The UN Convention on the Rights of the Child (1989, Article 23) states that disabled children have the right to a "full and decent life, in conditions which ensure dignity, promote self-reliance and facilitate the child's active participation in the community".

Right to develop friendships and relationships and to participate in ordinary leisure and recreational activities

The children and young people we spent time with had limited opportunities for developing friendships and relationships. But having friends is as important for them as for any children. It was also clear that this group of children and young people wanted to do the sorts of *ordinary* things that all children do, not necessarily activities that were *specially designed* for them.

The UN Convention on the Rights of the Child (1989, Article 31) recognises the rights of all children to rest and leisure, and to engage in play and recreational activities that are age and culturally appropriate. Member states have a responsibility to respect and promote the right of the child to participate fully in cultural and artistic life, and to

encourage the provision of appropriate and equal opportunities for cultural, artistic, recreational and leisure activity.

Right to be consulted and informed about their care and support

Despite the fact that the children and young people we spent time with were often in contact with very large numbers of professionals, there was little real evidence of effective consultation between the multi-agency services and disabled children with complex health care needs about their care and support. Even where families had access to a keyworker, we did not get a strong sense that there were many primary relationships between this person and the children themselves. A close relationship with a keyworker could give an opportunity for young people to be more involved with their care and allow them to have a voice. As Stalker et al (2003) recommend:

> The wider development of key worker systems would be beneficial for all children, especially those who have complex needs. Regular contact should be maintained between key workers and the young person and her family. (Stalker et al, 2003, p 142)

The UN Convention on the Rights of the Child (1989, Article 12) makes member states responsible for ensuring that any child who is capable of forming their own views has the right to express those views freely in all matters affecting them, and that the views of the child should be given due weight in accordance with the age and maturity of the child. Listening to children, and promoting the active involvement of children and young people in planning and delivering services and support to meet their real needs, are key elements of recent and current UK policy development. The recently established Children and Young People's Unit has published an action plan for children and young people's participation which sets out the English government's commitment to a set of core principles for enabling children and young people to take part in the planning, delivery and evaluation of government policy and services. The Quality Protects Programme, part of the English government's strategy for tackling social exclusion of disadvantaged and vulnerable children, promotes the active involvement of children and young people as one of its five key work-programme themes. In addition, the Department of Health's document on principles for involving children and young people in the NHS (DoH, 2002) gives many examples of the benefits of including young people and how this can help to develop services that will be better designed to met their needs.

Summary

- *Communication* – more than half of the disabled children and young people with whom we spent time had no verbal communication. Some of these children used signs, but not all had a recognised, individualised means of communicating with others. In Chapter 4, we saw that several families were keen to support their child to develop a communication system, but that some had found it difficult to receive prompt, appropriate help from the multi-agency service with this. Time spent with children and young people highlighted their desire to express their social and emotional needs and wishes, including outlets for communicating pain and distress associated with complex health care interventions themselves.

- *Primary carers* – most of the children we spent time with lived with their birth parents, but in four families, foster parents, grandparents and an adoptive parent, were caring for children. It is important for multi-agency services to consider the sorts of pressures that lead to children with complex health care needs being cared for outside their birth families, and whether support to foster and adoptive families is adequate.

- *Independence* – the vast majority of children and young people we spent time with had close, but extremely dependent relationships with their parents or carers. Children and young people were reliant on their family, and other adult carers, not only to support them with their complex health care needs and personal care, but also to support them in every other area of their lives. Very few children and young people could spend time alone with friends, or begin to develop some independence away from close family members. One or two families (quoted in Chapter 4) talked about how they were trying to find ways to support their children with complex health care needs to have more independence, but admittedly

this was a very difficult area for parents and carers to consider, given the degree of their involvement with their child's daily care and support.

- *Friendships, relationships and access to leisure* – the children and young people we spent time with had limited opportunities for developing friendships and relationships, although children with verbal communication were more likely to have significant friendships underlining the importance of support for communication. It was also clear that this group of children and young people wanted to do the sorts of *ordinary* things that all children do, not necessarily activities that were *specially designed* for them.

- *Relationships with professionals* – despite the fact that the children and young people we spent time with were often in contact with very large numbers of professionals, they were very accepting of this, and appreciated it if professionals took time to get to know them. However, there was little real evidence of effective consultation between the multi-agency services and disabled children with complex health care needs about their care and support. Even where families had access to a keyworker, we did not get a strong sense that there were strong relationships between this person and the children themselves. Some children were unaware of the identity of their keyworker even when named and described. A close relationship with a keyworker could give an opportunity for young people to be more involved with their care and allow them to have a voice.

7

Conclusions and recommendations

Chapter 1 set out a list of success factors for multi-agency working, drawn from the well-established body of literature that already exists on this topic. In this final chapter, we return to those factors and summarise issues relating to the process and impact of multi-agency working in services to disabled children with complex health needs. We also make recommendations for those involved in the policy and practice of multi-agency working for this group of children, based on the findings of the research reported here.

Pooling and sharing the resources needed to work together

There were many, and varied, arrangements for defining and organising the resources needed to work together. Although one site had managed to establish a multi-agency approach to resource sharing at strategic and operational level, none of the sites had found a way to pool mainstream budgets. Half of the multi-agency services we visited were funded on a short-term basis and consequently their longevity as established services was not assured. Many professionals also voiced concerns that funding was inadequate for providing both effective management and administration of the service as a whole, and for providing the level of support required by families and children with complex health care needs who were eligible for the service.

The lack of clear, adequate and agreed funding routes meant that eligibility to the service had been restricted in some places. Despite the supposed focus on working together, funding disputes were still commonplace, and were a great source of distress

when played out in front of families. A lack of clarity about either the future funding of the multi-agency service, or responsibility for funding operational aspects (such as care packages) meant that commitment from professionals (to partnership working) was compromised, and families were left uncertain about the nature and extent of their entitlements.

Recommendations:

- *Dedicated resources* are needed to support the management and administrative functions of multi-agency working. Lead professionals should not be expected to implement and manage change without protected time and funding for this role.
- Individual agencies' commitment to partnership working should be underpinned by a *resource contribution to the multi-agency service*. The nature and extent of this contribution should be clearly documented from the outset, and *championed* by senior managers where necessary.
- More attention should be paid to the potential of using Health Act *flexibilities* to support multi-agency working.

The rationale and aims of multi-agency working

The rationale for multi-agency working was not always clear to those involved. If professionals are not clear about why multi-agency working is important, then they are less likely to be committed to the process of working together, particularly when problems or difficulties arise. Partnership with families in terms of planning and developing the multi-agency services was low, and this was evident in the fact that two services had been developed primarily in response to service pressures and the demands of professionals, rather than in response to an awareness of the needs of local families. Similarly, there were different levels of understanding and commitment to the aims of the different multi-agency services. A lack of clarity from professionals about the primary purpose of a multi-agency service will leave families unclear about what the service can offer them and what their expectations of it should be.

Recommendations:

- *Bringing about better outcomes for service users* should be the central rationale for any new multi-agency service that aims to support disabled children with complex health care needs and their families. Without a clear understanding of how the partnership will make a positive difference for families and children, commitment from professionals will flounder.
- As already noted by previous research (see Chapter 1), there is a *need for explicit agreement and commitment to a clear, shared vision that defines the purpose of multi-agency working.* Individuals involved in the multi-agency process need time, space and information to enable them to consider the question 'Why work in partnership?' and to use this understanding to challenge their own, and others', lack of commitment where necessary.
- Professionals and agencies need to have a *clear understanding and commitment to the aims of the partnership.* It is helpful to clarify and document what this commitment entails, in practice, for agencies and individual professionals. Attention should be paid to promoting and maintaining commitment to the aims of the multi-agency working in the longer term as well as at the initial stages of a setting up a new service.

Different models of multi-agency working and the nature of services provided to families

Each of the six sites operated a different form of multi-agency working and provided a slightly different nature of service to families and children. There were, however, three common elements across the six sites: coordinating administration; coordinating services and support; and, providing services and support. Coordination of services and support to families was achieved through the provision of a keyworker. Just one of the six sites was providing a service that coordinated both administration and services and support (through a key worker scheme), as well as acting as a direct service provider. Our findings showed that there were no significant differences between service models in terms of their overall impact of either families' access to services, or family quality of life.

There was a small amount of evidence, however, to suggest that access was improved as a result of contact with a keyworker whose role encompassed working together with families to establish their needs for services and support. Although not statistically significant (as numbers are too small), when answers to the question about access to services were summed across sites, it appeared that the only two sites where access was mostly easier (as opposed to the same, worse, or unknown) were both sites providing service coordination. However, in terms of the other sites, it appeared that the basic problem of inadequate provision of services in many areas simply cancelled out any attempts to improve access through a more coordinated approach.

Similarly, it is interesting to note that when answers to the question about impact on quality of life were summed across sites, it appeared that the three sites where families reported that their quality of life was mostly better (as opposed to the same, worse or unknown) were again all sites where families had access to a keyworker to coordinate their services and support.

Across all sites there was a lack of clarity about basic elements of the multi-agency service and how these operated, including confusion from families about the role of their keyworker. As already noted, a lack of clarity about how a service operates and what it offers will leave families unclear about their entitlements and expectations.

None of the multi-agency services appeared to be able to provide a single point of contact for families. Despite the fact that more than half of the families we interviewed had access to a keyworker with a specific remit to coordinate services for them, very few families felt that they were receiving a coordinated service and most families felt that they were still taking on the role of keyworker themselves. Families did not appear to have access to regular reviews of their needs, or to have a clear picture of their entitlements. There was also evidence that families were still experiencing multiple assessments and reviews, and the provision of a keyworker did not have a significant impact on resolving this duplication.

None of the six multi-agency services appeared to offer a truly flexible and responsive approach to child and family need. Most sites were constrained by budgets, staffing levels and waiting lists in their ability to respond flexibly to the real needs of local children and families. And a lack of regular, consistent reviews offered little scope for responding to the changing needs of families and children over time.

Across all sites there was little evidence of Black and minority ethnic families accessing the multi-agency services. Nor was there evidence of proactive work by professionals to target families from Black and minority ethnic groups or to make the service more accessible to them.

Recommendations:

- To reiterate the findings of previous research, *good multi-agency working requires a clearly defined structure*, or model, to explain how the multi-agency process will operate, particularly in terms of the nature of work with children and families and the expected outcomes for them. The model of the service should be clearly documented for professionals and made available to families in an appropriate format.
- *Families need clarity about their entitlements and expectations* with regard to a multi-agency service. Professionals too need information (that they can refer back to) to help them understand how things operate. A service leaflet or handbook can be helpful, but attention should be paid to publicising the existence of such information and keeping it up to date.
- *Providing a single, human, point of contact for families* should be a central component of any multi-agency service. However, the mere presence of a keyworker is not in itself enough. Attention needs to be paid to clarifying the nature of this person's

role and responsibilities, particularly in terms of coordinating, reducing duplication, and facilitating better access to services and support.
- Multi-agency services should be able to *respond to families' real, cultural and changing needs*. Services need to think proactively about how to engage with families as a whole, and with those who do not currently use the service. They also need to consider how to engage with families from Black and minority ethnic groups and to monitor service access and take-up by these families. A purely individualistic approach to service provision, based on one-by-one assessments of the needs of individual families and children will not provide a broader sense of the wider issues for local (and prospective) users of the service. Partnership with families is key here, alongside a recognition of the importance of service monitoring and evaluation.

Roles, responsibilities and contributions of the professionals involved in the multi-agency process

Each multi-agency service was composed of project managers, senior managers, and direct care and support staff. Each of these groups had important and varied roles and responsibilities. The role of project manager was largely similar across the six sites and was characterised by a demanding and heavy workload. Almost without exception, project managers had the closest grasp of operational and strategic issues in the service, and were the only professionals who could take a macro- and micro-view of the way the service impacted on children, families, other professionals and individual agencies. Most project managers also retained operational responsibility for some family casework, in addition to their strategic and management responsibilities, and showed an incredible commitment to the families for whom they were directly and indirectly responsible. Although they had a clear understanding of their roles, the broad and open-ended nature of these responsibilities had a negative impact on the personal health and well-being of several project managers we interviewed.

Senior managers and direct care and support staff were less clear about what their roles and responsibilities entailed in respect of their involvement with the multi-agency services. Senior managers offered support and resources to services and their presence at multi-agency meetings was perceived as a marker of an agency's commitment to the partnership. Individual senior managers, however, lacked clarity about the operational and management details of the multi-agency services and did not appear to show sustained commitment in terms of their agencies' accountability for the overall effectiveness of the service.

Direct care and support staff acted as the main link between the multi-agency service and families and children, and offered a range of therapies, advice and input. Many of these professionals were also taking on the role of keyworker for children and families. It was interesting to note that despite concerns from senior managers, multi-agency working did not appear to have a detrimental impact on the workload of professionals. The boundaries of this role were universally blurred, which meant that individual professionals interpreted the nature of their duties in different ways, leading to inequalities in service provision. Consequently, many families were unsure about their entitlement to a keyworker and what this person could offer them in the way of support.

There was some evidence of role expansion, particularly for those health professionals who had begun to take on a more generic role as a keyworker. This had two outcomes. First, given the large number of health professionals who were already involved in the lives of disabled children with complex health care needs and their families, there was a tendency for health issues to predominate, to the exclusion of support for social and emotional issues. Second, some social care professionals (social workers in particular) felt that their roles had been eroded in what they perceived to be a medically dominated arena. The input of other key staff (such as education professionals) also appeared to be *missing* from multi-agency assessments and meetings. The focus on offering multi-agency support to children with *health care* needs tended to be about supporting the child to stay alive, be at home and attend school on a regular basis. These are important outcomes, but their achievement predominated to the extent that some professionals questioned whether the social model of disability had been forgotten for this group of children and families. The findings from families

and children clearly echo this, and remind us that health care needs are an important, but small, aspect of overall human quality of life.

Recommendations:

- As stated in Chapter 1, the roles, responsibilities and contributions of people involved in the multi-agency process should be clarified and documented from the start. The nature of multi-agency working can be all encompassing and the agencies involved have a responsibility to ensure that a few key staff (such as project managers) are not overloaded by a personal responsibility for all aspects of the multi-agency service, particularly when the roles of others involved are not clear. *More clarity about roles* should also ensure more equitable service provision for families and children.
- Multi-agency services for children with complex health care needs should *take care that the input of health professionals does not predominate* in the operational and strategic development of the service. Participation of staff from all agencies involved (including social care and education professionals) is essential, as is an awareness that support for social and emotional needs is as vital as support for health care needs.

Leadership, allies and champions

Many of the professionals we interviewed explicitly acknowledged the importance of networking and alliances. They felt that the formal structures established by the multi-agency services, to bring people together on a more regular basis and with a specific focus, had been helpful in forging and developing relationships within and across agencies.

However, it appeared that in all of the six sites, the main leader and *champion* for multi-agency working was the project manager of the service. We identified little evidence of effective leadership for the multi-agency services among senior managers, although they acted as sometime allies and champions when needed. It was not clear whether there was a sustained commitment to the multi-agency service from *all* agencies involved.

The majority of the project managers we interviewed were all characterised by their drive and commitment to improving outcomes for families. For them, this was the *raison-d'être* of the multi-agency service and was all the evidence they needed to champion its cause. Most direct care and support staff also *championed* the multi-agency service in that they expressed a great deal of enthusiasm for partnership working and showed commitment to action for families and attending joint meetings. It is interesting to note, however, that their commitment tended to focus on the positive outcomes for themselves as professionals, rather than any link between multi-agency working and better outcomes for families.

The reliance on one key champion (in this case at middle-management level) can mean that there is a fragility of commitment to the ethos of multi-agency working and that commitment could very easily be eroded if the key champion leaves or moves on. It can also mean that the service may not be actively championed at strategic and operational levels, leaving its aim and purpose open to challenge and misinterpretation.

Recommendations:

- Multi-agency services should acknowledge the *importance of establishing and supporting champions at different levels* within different agencies. Resources should be set aside with the specific aim of creating opportunities for networking and building alliances and relationships.
- The *reliance on one key champion and leader should be avoided at all costs*. Aside from the negative personal impact for the individual concerned, there is also a real risk that the service will flounder, or commitment be significantly eroded should this person leave or move on to a different role. The importance of succession planning is also important here and can be a good way to build additional champions for the service.
- Multi-agency services should *refocus on building commitment to achieving outcomes for families*. Research (Townsley et al, 2002) has established that professionals often need to see evidence of success before they will sign up their commitment to a new initiative, such as multi-agency working for disabled children with complex health care needs. Again, the importance of partnership with families and monitoring outcomes is important

here, in order to provide evidence (or not) that multi-agency working is effective for families as well as professionals themselves.

Learning, support and supervision

Working in multi-agency services provided professionals with enhanced opportunities for personal and professional development. Staff said they learnt more about each other's roles and as a result felt more efficient in meeting families' needs. There was evidence of excellent shared training between health and other agencies on supporting children's health needs in the community. However, it appeared that although learning opportunities were better overall, there was insufficient training on specific aspects of multi-agency working such as what it meant to be a keyworker, how to chair meetings, and so on. The impact for families was that although professionals were better equipped to meet children's health care needs, they were less successful at other aspects of their multi-agency role, such as service coordination, family advocacy and paying attention to the needs of the child and family as a whole.

In terms of support and supervision, multi-agency meetings were highlighted as an important way for direct care and support staff to give and receive peer support and supervision, and as a way to share and discuss joint issues and problems. However, it appeared that there was often a lack of support from managers in professionals' own agencies. Professionals were very positive about the support they received from the project manager of the multi-agency service, but routinely cited instances of indifferent or poor support from their own line managers. This included being expected to fill service gaps at short notice. There did not seem to be clear guidelines for all staff on how much time commitment should be made available to the multi-agency service, which further compounded the lack of support for this aspect of their work by their own line managers. The impact for families was felt in terms of some professionals' uncertain commitment to attending meetings, regular communication, and building relationships with children and young people.

Recommendations:

- Multi-agency services for children with complex health care needs should pay attention to the *need to provide generic training on partnership working* and what it means for individuals and their agencies. A focus on providing training on how best to support children's health care needs is essential, but should not overshadow other aspects of their care and support.
- *Multi-agency meetings* should be recognised as a popular and effective forum for peer support between professionals. Managers may want to consider providing additional opportunities for professionals to get together, such as action learning groups, or regular professional-led open workshops on specific topics. As suggested in Chapter 1, learning should be ongoing and a reflective approach fostered to enable continuous improvement as the process develops.
- *Support from managers and agencies* is vital for those staff directly involved in partnership work, particularly where workloads or job descriptions are affected. Project managers should work with managers in individual agencies to gain their commitment to the ethos of multi-agency working, and by extension, commitment to releasing their staff on a regular basis for their work on the multi-agency service.

Management and accountability

Across all the sites there was a lack of clarity about management and accountability arrangements. Two sites had not established any formal management arrangements, but even in the four sites where multi-agency management groups existed, the role and decision-making powers of these groups were unclear. There were concerns about the composition of the groups, especially in relation to including both parents and professionals who could commit their agencies' financial resources. Partly as a result of this there was also a lack of clarity about who was ultimately accountable for strategic decision making for the multi-agency service as a whole, and for individual families, given the multi-agency context.

The impact of this confusion was that most professionals felt that ultimate accountability for the service and for families lay with project managers.

Project managers concurred with this, and it was clear that such a high level of responsibility had added to the significant pressure of their already heavy and demanding workloads. We would question whether project managers, as middle managers, were really the most appropriate people to be responsible for such a significant level of accountability, especially given the lack of commitment to the service from more senior managers within separate agencies. We were concerned that project managers were left to shoulder an unacceptable, and unwarranted level of accountability without clear support or line management.

For families, uncertainty about service accountability left them in *shifting sands*, as responsibility for different aspects of a multi-agency service was attributed to different agencies. This exacerbated the inability of multi-agency services to provide a single point of contact, particularly if difficulties arose, or families wished to make complaints. In addition, the lack of someone at the centre of the management structure who was able to commit resources meant that there were long delays on decisions about aspects of service provision for families, particularly in terms of funding for larger items of equipment such as wheelchairs, or adaptations.

Recommendations:

- All multi-agency services should establish *clear and documented arrangements for management and accountability*. These should be communicated in writing to all those involved in the service so that professionals and agencies are clear about where their own responsibilities begin and end.
- A *governance structure* that ensures open, active and effective, shared decision making should be established. This should clarify who is ultimately responsible for making final decisions about different types of strategic and operational issues, including funding for care packages. Such a structure may involve setting up a multi-agency management group. If this is the case, then the role and status of the group should be agreed and documented, and its decision-making powers clarified if particular people are absent from meetings (this might include delegated decision making if purse-holders cannot attend).

- *Project managers, or middle managers, should not be held ultimately accountable* for the multi-agency service that they manage. Alternative arrangements for accountability should be established, and this might include a multi-agency management group taking on agreed liability for the multi-agency service as a whole.

Communication

Services provided both formal and informal ways for staff to communicate and share information with each other. Professionals felt that communication was greatly improved by working in a multi-agency context in that there were now clearer and more efficient channels for information sharing. Although communication between and within direct care and support staff, and project managers was good, it was less effective between the support staff and senior managers, which meant that vital and helpful insights relating to work with families were not always relayed *upwards*.

Professionals believed that multi-agency working had enhanced communication between themselves and families. They expressed the view that since their working practices were now easier and more efficient (particularly in terms of communicating with professionals from other agencies), that this, in itself, meant they were providing a better service to children and families. And yet families expressed the opposite view. They were not wholly positive about communication between professionals and themselves, nor did they perceive that professionals were working together and communicating better. This seems to highlight the point that families have little interest in what happens *behind the scenes* in terms of service efficiency. For them, the proof of action by professionals is better access to services, more coordination of their *own* support, and more attention to the multi-faceted process of family and child quality of life. Simply being aware that multi-agency working enabled professionals to find things out quickly and more easily was not necessarily a boon for families, unless it resulted in more effective services and support for them.

Problems still existed around the incompatibility of IT systems. In addition, concerns (data protection, confidentiality, permission from families) about sharing databases hindered the effective sharing of records and data. Formal hand-held records for families had only been developed by one site, but some families felt that they still had to take responsibility for ensuring that some professionals completed these. Interviews with families also indicated that there was continuing duplication in terms of assessments and reviews, and that no one agency, or indeed the multi-agency service, appeared to be taking an overview of this.

Recommendations:

- *Good communication* between all those involved in a multi-agency service is essential. It was positive to see evidence of this, and of the establishment of structures for effective communication between professionals. Multi-agency services should recognise the importance of developing and maintaining this aspect of the multi-agency process, and continue their efforts to make use of opportunities for sharing information. Senior managers should recognise the important insights that direct care and support staff can contribute to service development and facilitate opportunities to listen to what they have to say.
- *Professionals should acknowledge the important role that good communication plays* in terms of service efficiency. However, they should also recognise that better outcomes for them do not necessarily result in better outcomes for families.
- *Common assessment tools and arrangements* for shared access to records are a vital part of ensuring a truly multi-agency approach to service provision. Care should be taken, however, to ensure that these really do replace existing arrangements, and do not simply add yet another layer of duplication for families.

Partnership with families

By partnership with families we mean ways in which professionals and the multi-agency service listened to and respected the views of families and children, and adopted a *whole family* approach to service provision, both in terms of regular contact and in terms of more formalised methods for consultation.

Findings from families did not appear to show significant evidence of *proactive, regular* contact with professionals. Nor did there seem to be much evidence of a whole family approach – rather the mother was the main focus for contact, with siblings and other family members being marginalised by multi-agency services. Despite this, families were generally positive about the experience of being listened to, and having their views as individual care-givers valued by professionals from the six multi-agency services. However, family involvement in more formalised consultation, such as in planning, developing and evaluating services was fairly ad hoc and lacked clarity of purpose to the families who did take part. The focus on an individualised approach to consultation simply offered individual solutions to family concerns, rather than providing professionals with a broader sense of the wider issues facing local families.

We were concerned that the process of consulting families appeared, in some sites, to be more about *rubber-stamping* existing practice, rather than offering real opportunities for feedback and change. Professionals at several sites presented the idea of partnership as a means by which they could be more transparent to families, particularly in terms of limits to resources and possibilities, and 'help them to realise' the limitations of the multi-agency service, rather than its potential to improve outcomes in new ways. Needless to say, such an approach is likely to demoralise families and discourages them from future participation in service planning and development. Findings showed that the more recently established services were better at practising partnership with families, indicating perhaps that involvement is most authentic at the start of a new service, or when something is being promoted as a new option. Longer-term services might have to work harder to make partnership with families authentic, since change is more difficult to consider and implement when procedures have been embedded for longer.

Consultation of any kind with disabled children and young people with complex health care needs was almost non-existent. This reflects wider research findings on consultation with disabled children (see Morris, 2002, for a guide on working with disabled children with communication impairments). However, the fact that so few, if any, children and young people had a relationship with, or even recognised, their keyworker was a surprising finding, and a lost opportunity for the multi-agency services.

A close relationship with a keyworker could give an opportunity for children and young people to be more involved with their care and allow them to have more of a voice. The time spent by the research team with children and young people highlighted their desire to express their social and emotional needs and wishes, including outlets for communicating pain and distress associated with complex health care interventions themselves. It also highlighted that for the majority of children and young people, some very basic human rights (right to communicate, right to independence, right to develop friendships and relationships, right to be consulted and informed) were being denied. Professionals felt that getting to know children and young people was a *luxury* that limited time and resources did not justify. They talked about barriers to communication and a lack of training. Parents also cited these barriers, but they had not prevented them from developing extraordinarily supportive and engaging relationships with their children.

Recommendations:

- Multi-agency providers should find *multiple ways to engage with families and disabled children* with complex health care needs. This includes partnership with individual parents, children, siblings and wider family members, both in terms of regular contact and in terms of more formalised methods for consultation, such as involvement in the planning, development and evaluation of the service.
- It is important to keep the *real needs of families and children at the forefront of the multi-agency process*. Professionals involved in multi-agency services need to take a broader approach to finding out what local families want and to consider the themes that emerge from consultation with families as a group, in addition to listening to and valuing the experiences of individual parents.
- Multi-agency services should *consider what they wish to achieve by partnership*, and be honest about this with families. Are parents ever going to have power to effect change? Or are they just there to agree things that have already been decided? Effective partnership, as opposed to tokenistic involvement, is about accepting that change is possible and that the process of listening to families involves a responsibility towards

considering alternative outcomes, not just justifying what already happens.

- Professionals, particularly those taking on the role of a named person, or service coordinator, must begin to *find ways to engage with disabled children and young people* with complex health care needs. This might involve accepting that there will never be sufficient training or resources available and that some engagement is better than none.

Monitoring and evaluation

Systematic and regular monitoring and evaluation were lacking in each of the six multi-agency services. Where they existed, monitoring and evaluation were more commonly ad hoc activities, characterised, for example, by sporadic service audits, parental questionnaires and one-off external evaluations. Children and young people were rarely asked their views about the services they received, and feedback from monitoring and evaluation activities to either children or their families was rare.

It was interesting to note that when we asked professionals whether they thought the multi-agency service was making a difference to families, they were unable to provide any clear evidence of impact and outcomes. Families, on the other hand, were able to provide a wealth of evidence in answer to the same question and were mostly able to quantify how far they felt the multi-agency service had made a positive difference to their overall quality of life. Many of the families we spoke to had things they wanted to say about the service – positive and negative – and were frustrated by the lack of opportunity for more routine and formal consultation. This begs the question – 'If professionals do not have systems for monitoring the process of multi-agency working or for evaluating the outcomes for families, how can they tell if the multi-agency service is really making a difference to those families and children it was set up to support?'. And thus how can commissioners tell if the extra resources needed for effective multi-agency working are truly justified?

Recommendations:

- As stated in Chapter 1, all partnerships should have a means of *monitoring the process and measuring the impact* of their work. Partners should be involved in setting objectives and committed to achieving them.
- *Evaluation criteria* should be established to measure improvements in policy, practice and service-user satisfaction. But ultimately, better outcomes for families and children should be the goal of any multi-agency service designed to support them.

Timescales and future planning

Three of the multi-agency services were funded permanently, and as such were perceived as established services in their own right. The remaining three had all been funded initially on a pilot project basis, and had a more uncertain future long term.

A lack of certainty in some areas about the future of the multi-agency services was compounded by ongoing structural changes within organisations, and by wider developments such as planning for implementing new Children's Trusts. Professionals were not clear how these new developments would tie in with the existing multi-agency service or indeed what nature of adaptation would be needed to allow for effective integration. In addition, the majority of the multi-agency services we visited appeared to *stand alone*, and were not linked in with other (often numerous) local multi-agency initiatives. There were some examples of transfer of good practice within and between agencies. However, examples of duplication and disconnection between different multi-agency initiatives remained problematic.

Families too, were unclear about what might happen, if anything, in the future, and how this would impact on the services and support they received. Some families talked about receiving services and support from several different multi-agency initiatives, which had obvious implications for duplication of meetings, assessments and reviews.

Recommendations:

- Where multi-agency services are time-limited, a *clear plan should indicate what will happen next*, and how, if at all, new ways of working will be embedded into mainstream services. Professionals, families, and where possible children and young people, should be aware of the time-limited nature of the service and the likely impact on them, now, and in the future.
- Commissioners and policy makers should recognise that *setting up multi-agency working can take a lot of time*, particularly at the start. Change of this nature can take years, not months, to achieve satisfactory outcomes for those involved.

Conclusion: multi-agency working for disabled children with complex health care needs and their families – has it made a difference?

As we have seen, multi-agency working, as exemplified in the six services we visited, appeared to be providing focused and effective support to families in terms of managing their disabled children's complex health care needs at home. In addition, the health needs of this group of children appeared to be largely well met. All except one of the children included in this study were living at home, and all those who were of school age were attending a local school or nursery on a regular basis. These findings appear to indicate that multi-agency working is making a significant difference to this group of children, who in previous research, were shown to face barriers to being at home and accessing education.

However, a number of social and emotional barriers for families remained. Very many families experienced major difficulties with daily routines (such as sleeping), and with finding and organising social activities for themselves and disabled child. There was no evidence to suggest that their contact with the multi-agency services had enabled families to have better access to short breaks or sitting services to alleviate some of the pressure of being *on call* for 24 hours a day. Most families received no support with claiming benefits entitlements, despite the fact that three quarters of those interviewed were living on an income below the national average and a large

proportion found it difficult to find and keep paid work. Families also reported numerous sources of emotional pressure, some of which were directly related to a lack of coordinated and flexible support from the multi-agency services. Despite the provision, in four areas, of a keyworker, a large proportion of families still felt they had no one to turn to for emotional support.

The time we spent with disabled children and young people with complex health care needs demonstrated that despite good intentions by the six multi-agency services, this group of children were still experiencing multiple barriers to exercising some basic human rights. These included barriers to the right to communicate, the right to independence, the right to develop friendships and relationships, and to participate in ordinary leisure and recreational activities, and the right to be consulted and informed about their care and support.

In terms of families' contact with services, our findings showed that there were no significant differences between service models in terms of their overall impact of either families' access to services, or family quality of life. There was a small amount of evidence, however, to suggest that access to services and impact on quality of life were slightly improved in services where families had some contact with a keyworker. Despite the fact that over half of the families included in this study had access to a keyworker, most families still appeared to be doing their own service coordination. There was also evidence that families were still experiencing multiple assessments and reviews, and the provision of a keyworker did not have a significant impact on resolving this duplication. None of the six multi-agency services appeared to offer a truly flexible and responsive approach to child and family need. Most sites were constrained by budgets, staffing levels and waiting lists in their ability to respond flexibly to the real needs of local children and families. And a lack of regular, consistent reviews offered little scope for responding to the changing needs of families and children over time. Across all sites there was little evidence of Black and minority ethnic families accessing the multi-agency services. Nor was there evidence of proactive work by professionals to target families from Black and minority ethnics groups or to make the service more accessible to them.

And yet two thirds of the families we interviewed reported that the multi-agency service had made a positive difference to the overall quality of their lives. Not one family felt that quality of life for them and their child was *worse* as a direct result of their involvement in the multi-agency service.

To sum up, in a relatively short time-span, multi-agency working has brought about some very positive and significant changes for families and children in terms of health gains and improved access to education, and to support for health care needs at home. What is missing, however, is a wider appreciation of what still needs to be achieved in terms of social and emotional support for families, and in terms of facilitating basic human rights for children and young people.

Previous research into the process of multi-agency working tells us that effective partnerships take time and effort to achieve. The focus in the early stages of development is thus likely to be on the process itself, or the mechanics, of setting up and establishing multi-agency services. As with any new enterprise, those involved will need to feel confident that they have perfected at least some aspects of the process, before they can pay proper attention to its impact and outcomes. As less conscious attention is needed to get the process right, it becomes more embedded and *automatic*, thus leaving more *space* for focusing on better outcomes for families.

It seems important to build on the successes that have already been achieved by the committed and hard-working professionals involved in this study. There is still some way to go, but many significant and positive steps have already been taken. The time is now right for multi-agency services to build on their important work, the structure and process of multi-agency working, and develop an increased appreciation of impact and outcomes for families.

References

Abbott, D., Morris, J. and Ward, L. (2001) *The best place to be? Policy, practice and the experiences of residential school placements for disabled children*, York: York Publishing Services.

Alexander, H. and Macdonald, E. (2001) 'Evaluating policy-driven multi-agency partnership working: a cancer prevention strategy group and a multi-agency domestic abuse forum', UK Evaluation Society Annual Conference, 5-7 December, Belfast.

Atkinson, M., Wilkin, A., Stott, A., Doherty, P. and Kinder, K. (2002) 'Multi-agency working: a detailed study', *LGA Research Report 26*, Slough: National Foundation for Education Research.

Banks, P. (2002) *Partnerships under pressure*, London: King's Fund.

Beattie, A. (2000) *Service co-ordination: Professionals' views on the role of a multi-agency service co-ordinator for children with disabilities*, Birmingham: The Handsel Trust.

Beresford, B. (1995) *Expert opinions: A national survey of parents caring for a severely disabled child*, Bristol/York: The Policy Press/Joseph Rowntree Foundation.

Beresford, B. (1997) *Personal accounts: Involving disabled children in research*, London: The Stationery Office.

Beresford, B. and Oldman, C. (2000) *Making homes fit for children*, Bristol/York: The Policy Press/Joseph Rowntree Foundation.

Brown, B., Crawford, P. and Darongkamas, J. (2000) 'Blurred roles and permeable boundaries: the experience of multidisciplinary working in community mental health', *Health and Social Care in the Community*, vol 8, no 6, pp 425-35.

Cabinet Office (1999) *Modernising government (White Paper)*, London: The Stationery Office.

Care Co-ordination Network UK (2001) *Information sheet*, York: CCNUK

Chamba, R., Ahmad, W., Hirst, M., Lawton, D. and Beresford, B. (1999) *On the edge: Minority ethnic families caring for a severely disabled child*, Bristol/York: The Policy Press/Joseph Rowntree Foundation.

Children's Society (2001) *Ask us* (CD-ROM), London: Children's Society.

Cigno, K. and Gore, J. (1999) 'A seamless service: meeting the needs of children with disabilities through a multi-agency approach', *Child and Family Social Work*, vol 4, no 4, pp 325-35.

Davey, V. and Henwood, M. (2003) 'Loose connections', *Community Care*, 15-21 May, pp 40-1.

DES (Department for Education and Skills) (2003) *Every child matters* www.dfes.gov.uk/everychildmatters

DETR (Department of the Environment, Transport and the Regions) (1999) *A working definition of local authority partnerships*, www.detr.gov.uk

Dobson, B. and Middleton, S. (1998) *Paying to care: The cost of childhood disability*, York: York Publishing Services.

Dobson, B., Middleton, S. and Beardsworth, A. (2001) *The impact of childhood disability on family life*, York: York Publishing Services.

DoH (Department of Health) (1991) *The Children Act 1989: Guidance and regulations. Volume 6: Children with disabilities*, London: The Stationery Office.

DoH (1997) *The New NHS: Modern, dependable (White Paper)*, London: The Stationery Office.

DoH (1998) *Partnership in action (new opportunities for joint working between health and social services) – A discussion document*, London: DoH.

DoH (2001a) *Valuing People (White Paper)*, London: The Stationery Office.

DoH (2001b) *The Quality Protects programme: Transforming children's services 2002-03*, HSC 2001/ 20: LAC (2001)28, 17 October, London: DoH.

DoH (2002) *Listening, hearing, responding: Core principles for the involvement of children and young people*, London: DoH.

DoH and Public Services Productivity Panel (2000) *Working in partnership: Developing a whole systems approach*, London: DoH and HM Treasury.

Doyle, B. (1997) 'Transdisciplinary approaches to working with families', in B. Carpenter (ed) *Families in context: Emerging trends in family support and early intervention*, London: David Fulton Publishers Ltd.

Flint, J., Mullen, T. and Scott, S. (2001) *An assessment of multi-agency work in Barmulloch and West Dromoyne*, Edinburgh: Scottish Executive Central Research Unit.

Flynn, R. (2002) *Short breaks: Providing better access and more choice for black disabled children and their parents*, Bristol/York: The Policy Press/Joseph Rowntree Foundation.

Glaser, B. and Strauss, A. (1967) *The discovery of grounded theory*, Chicago, IL: Aldine.

Glendinning, C. (2002) 'Partnerships between health and social services: developing a framework for evaluation', *Policy & Politics*, vol 30, no 1, pp 115-27.

Glendinning, C., Kirk, S., Guiffridda, A. and Lawton, D. (1999) *The community-based care of technology-dependent children in the UK: Definitions, numbers and costs*, Manchester: National Primary Care Research and Development Centre, University of Manchester.

Hague, G. (2000) 'Reducing domestic violence … what works? Multi-agency fora, briefing note', *Crime reduction research series*, London: Home Office.

Harries, J., Gordon, P., Plamping, D. and Fischer, M. (1999) *Elephant problems and fixes that fail: The story of a search for new approaches to inter-agency working*, London: King's Fund.

Hart, S. (1991) 'The collaborative dimension: risks and rewards of collaboration', in C. McLauglin and M. Rouse (eds) *Supporting schools*, London: David Fulton.

Harvey, J. (1997) 'Translating the guidance into effective school policy', oral presentation to the South East Institute of Public Health conference on Medication in Schools, June, Birmingham.

Hudson, B., Hardy, B., Henwood, M. and Wistow, G. (1997) *Interagency collaboration: Draft final report*, Leeds: Nuffield Institute for Health.

Hudson, B., Hardy, B., Henwood, M. and Wistow, G. (1999) 'In pursuit of inter-agency collaboration in the public sector', *Public Management*, vol 1, no 2, pp 235-60.

Human Rights Act (1998) London: The Stationery Office.

Interconnections (2001) 'Service co-ordination opportunities within a single agency', unpublished working paper, Birmingham: Interconnections.

JRF (Joseph Rowntree Foundation) (1999) 'Supporting disabled children and their families', *Foundations* No 79, York: JRF.

Kagan, C., Lewis, S. and Heaton, P. (1998) *Caring to work: Accounts of working parents of disabled children*, London/York: Family Policy Studies Centre/ Joseph Rowntree Foundation.

Kelly, B., McColgan, M. and Scally, M. (2000) 'A chance to say – involving children who have learning disabilities in a pilot study on family support services', *Journal of Learning Disabilities*, vol 4, no 2, pp 115-27.

Kennedy, C., Lynch, E. and Goodlad, R. (2001) *Good practice in joint/multi-agency working on homelessness*, Edinburgh: Scottish Executive Central Research Unit.

Kerr, S.M. and Macintosh, J.B. (2000) 'Coping when a child has a disability: exploring the impact of parent-to-parent support', *Child: Care, Health and Development*, vol 26, no 4, pp 309-22.

Kirk, S. and Glendinning, C. (1999) *Supporting parents caring for a technology-dependent child*, Manchester: National Primary Care Research and Development Centre, University of Manchester.

Lacey, P. (1997) 'Multidisciplinary teamwork: practice and training', unpublished PhD thesis, Birmingham: School of Education, University of Birmingham.

Lacey, P. and Ouvry, C. (eds) (2000) *People with profound and multiple learning disabilities: A collaborative approach to meeting complex needs*, London: David Fulton Publishers.

Learning Disability Advisory Group (2001) *Fulfilling the promises: Proposals for a framework for services for people with learning difficulties*, Cardiff: National Assembly for Wales.

Leathard, A. (ed) (1994) *Going interprofessional: Working together for health and welfare*, London: Routledge.

Leeds Health Action Zone (2002) *Partnership self-assessment toolkit: A practical guide to creating and maintaining successful partnerships*, Leeds: Leeds Health Action Zone.

Limbrick-Spencer, G. (2000) *Parents' support needs: The views of parents of children with complex needs*, Birmingham: The Handsel Trust.

Lloyd, G., Stead, J. and Kendrick, A. (2001) *Hanging on in there: A study of inter-agency work to prevent school exclusion in three local authorities*, London: National Children's Bureau.

Mencap (2001) *Don't count me out: The exclusion of children with a learning disability from education because of health needs*, London: Mencap.

Mencap (2003) *Arts for all? The accessibility of arts and cultural venues for families with children with a learning disability*, London: Mencap.

Michaelis, C., Warzak, W., Stanek, K. and Van Riper, C. (1992) 'Parental and professionals perceptions of problems associated with long term pediatric home tube feeding', *Journal of the American Dietetic Association*, vol 92, no 10, pp 1235-8.

Mitchell, W. and Sloper, P. (2000) *User-friendly information for families with disabled children: Guide to good practice*, York: Joseph Rowntree Foundation.

Morris, J. (1999) *Hurtling into a void: Transition to adulthood for young disabled people with complex health and support needs*, Brighton: Pavilion.

Morris, J. (2002) *A lot to say! A guide for social workers, personal advisors and others working with disabled children and young people with communication impairments*, London: Scope (available free).

Mukherjee, S., Beresford, B. and Sloper, P. (1999) *Unlocking key working: An analysis and evaluation of key worker services for families with disabled children*, Bristol/York: The Policy Press/Joseph Rowntree Foundation.

Mukherjee, S., Sloper, P., Beresford, B. and Lund, P. (2000) *A resource pack: Developing a key worker service for families with a disabled child*, York: Social Policy Research Unit, University of York.

Murray, P. (2001) 'Access to inclusive leisure', *Network News* 3, August.

Noyes, J. (1999a) 'The views and experiences of young people who use assisted ventilation', *Findings,* No 969, York: Joseph Rowntree Foundation.

Noyes, J. (1999b) *Voices and choices: Young people who use assisted ventilation: Their health, social care and education*, London: The Stationery Office.

Oldman, C. and Beresford, B. (1998) *Homes unfit for children: Housing, disabled children and their families*, Bristol/York: The Policy Press/Joseph Rowntree Foundation.

ONS (Office for National Statistics) (2000) *Family spending: A report on the 1999-2000 family expenditure survey*, London: The Stationery Office.

Petr, C.G., Murdock, B. and Chapin, R. (1995) 'Home care for children dependent on medical technology: the family perspective', *Social Work in Pediatrics*, vol 21, no 1, pp 23-37.

Potter, C. and Whittaker, C. (2001) *Enabling communication in children with autism*, London: Jessica Kingsley.

Redmond, B. (2000) *The needs of carers of fragile babies and young children with severe developmental disability: Report summary, conclusions and recommendations*, Dublin: Centre for the Study of Developmental Disabilities and Department of Social Policy and Social Work, University of Dublin.

Revans, L. (2003) 'Pioneers together', *Community Care*, 3-9 April, pp 28-30.

Roberts, K. and Lawton, D. (2001) 'Acknowledging the extra care parents give their disabled children', *Child: Care, Health and Development*, vol 27, no 4, pp 307-19.

Robinson, C. and Jackson, P. (1998) *The role of children's hospices in the provision of short term care*, York: York Publishing Services.

Scottish Executive (2000) *The same as you? A review of services for people with learning disabilities*, Edinburgh: Scottish Executive.

Shakespeare, T., Priestley, M. and Barnes, C. (1999) *Life as a disabled child: A qualitative study of young people's experiences and perspectives*, Leeds: Disability Research Unit, University of Leeds.

Sloper, P. and Turner, S. (1992) 'Service needs of families of children with severe physical disability', *Child: Care, Health and Development*, vol 18, pp 259-82.

Sloper, P. (1999) 'Models of service support for parents of disabled children: what do we know?', *Child: Care, Health and Development*, vol 25, no 2, pp 85-99.

Snell, J. (2003) 'Do you speak my language?', *Community Care*, 27 Feb-5 March.

Stalker, K., Carpenter, J., Phillips, R., Connors, C., MacDonald, C., Eyre, J., Noyes, J., Chaplin, S. and Place, M. (2003) *Care and treatment? Supporting children with complex needs in health care settings*, Brighton: Pavilion.

Taylor, S. and Bogdan, R. (1984) *Introduction to qualitative research methods: The search for meaning*, New York, NY: John Wiley & Sons.

Townsley, R. and Robinson, C. (1999) 'More than just a health issue: a review of current issues in the care of enterally-fed children living in the community', *Health and Social Care in the Community*, vol 7, no 3, pp 216-24.

Townsley, R. and Robinson, C. (2000) *Food for thought: Effective support for families caring for a child who is tube-fed*, Bristol: Norah Fry Research Centre, University of Bristol.

Townsley, R., Howarth, J., Graham, M. and Le Grys, P. (2002) *Committed to change? Promoting the involvement of people with learning difficulties in staff recruitment*, Bristol/York: The Policy Press/Joseph Rowntree Foundation.

Tozer, R. (1999) *At the double: Supporting families with two or more severely disabled children*, London: National Children's Bureau.

Triangle (2001) *Two way street: Training video and handbook about communicating with disabled children and young people*, Brighton: Triangle.

Turnbull, H., Summers, J., Poston, D. and Beegle, G. (2000) 'Enhancing family quality of life through partnerships and core concepts of disability policy', Paper presented to the 11th International Association of the Scientific Study of International Disability World Congress, 29-31 July, Seattle, WA, US.

UN Convention on the Rights of the Child (1989) *UN General Assembly Document A/RES/44/25*.

Wagner, J., Power, E. J. and Fox, H. (1988) *Technology-dependent children: Hospital versus home care*, Philadelphia, PA: JP Lippincott.

Watson, D., Townsley, R., Abbott, D. and Latham, P. (2002) 'Working together? Multi-agency working in services to disabled children with complex health care needs and their families', *A Literature Review*, Birmingham: Handsel Trust.

Wilcock, H., Armstrong, J., Cottee, S., Neale, G. and Elia, M. (1991) 'Artificial nutritional support for patients in the Cambridge health district', *Health Trends*, vol 23, pp 93-100.

Wray, J., Brettle, A., Long, A. and Grant, M. (2001) 'What the papers say about multi-professional working: a review', *Transforming Health Care Through Research, Education and Technology Conference*, Dublin, 16 November.

Young, R., Hardy, B., Waddington, E. and Jones, N. (2003) 'Wales slays the critics', *Community Care*, 12-18 June, pp 40-1.